Innocence and Experience

Innocence and Experience,

Stuart Hampshire, 1914 -

Harvard University Press
Cambridge, Massachusetts
1989

Library of Congress Cataloging-in-Publication Data
Hampshire, Stuart, 1914–
Innocence and experience / Stuart Hampshire.
p.   cm.
Includes index.
ISBN 0-674-45448-0 (alk. paper)
1. Political ethics.   I. Title.
JA79.H264   1989
172—dc19   89-31195

Acknowledgments

Almost the whole of this book was written in the Wissenschaftskolleg zu Berlin during the academic year 1987–88, which I spent in Berlin while my wife, Nancy Cartwright, was a Fellow of that institution. I wish to thank the Director, Wolf Lepenies, and Reinhardt Prosser for providing me with a room in which for several months I could be free from all distractions. I am grateful to the many other members of the Kolleg who made that year so enjoyable. I am grateful to the faculty, graduates, and undergraduates of the Department of Philosophy at Stanford University for the stimulus that I have received while being privileged to serve as emeritus professor for some years after my retirement elsewhere. I am very grateful to Patricia Williams of Harvard University Press for the repeated encouragement, practical advice, and help which have propelled me forward; also to two readers for Harvard University Press, and to my editor, Jennifer Snodgrass, for some most helpful advice on presentation. I wish to thank Dorothy Franklin, who gallantly typed a manuscript which was certainly not easy.

Contents

Introduction   1

1. Parts of the Soul   21

Reason and the Soul   30
Justice and the Soul   32
Thought and Reflection   38
Reason and Imagination   41
Language and Knowledge   44

2. Justice and History   49

Practical Reasoning   51
Procedural Justice and Historical Possibility   54
Reply to Relativism   62
Nazism and Evil   66
Basic Procedural Justice   72

3. Hume's Ghost   79

False Isolation   83
Value Judgments   88
Possibilities and Presuppositions   93
Fact and Value   95
Kinds of Possibility   99
Good and Evil Again   105
Procedural Justice: A Summary   107
Hume's Last Reply   109

4. *Individuality and Memory* 111

Memory and Variety 114
Individuals and History 119
Imagination 125
Transcendence 131
Virtue and Justice 134
The Dual Aspect of Morality 136
Justice and Pluralism 137
Justice and Liberal Assumptions 142
Attachment to the Past 146
Conflicts about Duty 153
Conceptions of the Good: Nietzsche 156

5. *Morality and Machiavelli* 159

Machiavelli's Problem 162
Towards a Reply 168
Innocence and Experience Illustrated 172
History Again 177
Justice and the Dispossessed 183
A Reply to Machiavelli 186

Index 191

Innocence and Experience

Introduction

❡ There are a thousand or more themes that might be pursued under the heading of moral and political philosophy. The whole of human life and of human history is open for inspection and evaluation under the title of moral philosophy. The particular philosophical preoccupations of this particular time compress the area and make the subject more manageable. But in this part of philosophy strictly philosophical interests can be expected to fall short in determining the issues to be pursued and the difficulties to be emphasised. The experience and the interests of the author unavoidably play a part, and for two reasons. First, he will feel at ease in writing about those aspects of common experience which he knows at first hand. Second, his experience will normally have left him with particular doubts and uncertainties, and these, when pressed and probed far enough, will turn into philosophical doubts and philosophical uncertainties. His experience will usually have left him with some particular philosophical bias. He will pick out the themes that recall points of stress and of conflict in his own past and in his own thought. It is reasonable that this bias should be made explicit. Having some fragments of biographical information, the reader will be better able to understand why one particular set of themes has been pursued and others neglected.

In the winters of 1930 and 1931 a middle-class family, mother, father, I, and my two brothers, would on some occasions leave the Adelphi Hotel in Liverpool after having lunch and come down the steps into Lime Street, where we would pass numbers of elderly women standing in the street and wearing shawls to keep out the cold and offering small sprigs of white heather to passers-by. These were the years of the world-wide depression; in 1930 I was sixteen and still at boarding school. The women begging in Lime Street were evidently very poor and they were badly clothed. The hotel was at that time a place of luxury. Driving home to North Wales we would pass through the empty and rather desolate streets of Birkenhead. Most of the ship-building and ship-repairing yards along the river Mersey were closed. Knots of men stood at the corners of the streets wearing mufflers and stamping their feet for warmth, having nothing to do. This was a usual scene in the northern industrial cities of Britain at that time. The unemployed had nowhere to go, and many of them were likely to remain unemployed for many years, perhaps permanently, unless there was another world war, which obviously would create a demand for ships to be built in Britain. Relief from unemployment for ship-builders and miners, and for many other workers in Britain, Europe, and America, came to seem more and more likely from 1933 onwards, when the likelihood of war was steadily increasing. It was repeatedly demonstrated, both in the thirties and later, that re-armament, a self-liquidating form of public works, was the most dependable cure for unemployment in industrial countries.

From 1933, when Hitler came to power in Germany, until 1936, I was an undergraduate at Balliol College, Oxford, and at school I had decided that philosophy was my main interest and contemporary politics second. It was difficult for undergraduates then not to think about the world-wide recession, of the throwing of coffee into the sea and of the destruction of food while there was hunger among the unemployed and their children in industrial cities everywhere. Children without shoes in the winter streets were not an unusual sight, and the shoe manufacturers were dismissing their workers because they could not sell their shoes. At the same time Hitler was drastically reducing unemployment in Germany while pursuing his previously announced programme of world conquest. In these circumstances it was natural to speculate that capitalism had entered a phase of increasing irrationality leading to some final self-destruction in total war. That recurring word "total" expresses much that is typical and horrible in the twentieth century. Even in the thirties one already had to look at the whole interconnected world, and not at those relatively few sheltered corners in which irrelevant and undisturbed ways of life might be continuing safely, as sheltered corners had persisted in the Roman Empire under the Antonines, or in eighteenth-century Europe.

Two other elements have to be added to the moral preoccupations of these pre-war years, which many undergraduates recognised to be pre-war years. First, theories of historical development, of which Marxism was only one specimen, still played a large part in political thinking, as they had done in the nineteenth century, often as theories of progress. Such theories of history had not been discredited, as they have been now, by the repeated failures of their predictions. University students often thought that they ought to be able to discern, and to choose, their future roles in a declining capitalism. "Which side are you on?" was constantly asked, with an accompanying assumption that it was already evident what the sides would soon turn out to be.

The second influence on my moral ideas, as they developed, was the sordid behaviour of the leading politicians in Britain confronting Nazism in Germany and Fascism elsewhere, particularly in Spain and Italy. It became obvious that they were ready to tolerate Fascist outrages and threats, and even to curry favour with Fascists, for the sake of protecting private property, which was threatened by the anticipated spread of Communism and of Socialism throughout Europe. I could observe this servility of Conservatives in the face of Fascism at first-hand, because I had become a colleague at All Souls' College, Oxford, of some of the leading appeasers of Hitler. This observation reinforced the tendency to ask "Which side are you on?"—a fatally over-simple question, as was later proved. Like many students at the time I knew that I was not on the side of the British Conservatives and I also knew that I never would be. For most Conservatives love of property, and of the secure possession of wealth, easily outweighed all other moral commitments.

Among many of those who distrusted and despised Conservative policies, Marxism came to seem plausible before 1939, because it offered an explanation both of Conservative policy towards Fascism and of the co-existence of poverty and overproduction, all within a single comprehensive theory. It seemed to have predicted both the evident irrationalities of capitalism and the accelerating nationalism and militarism which would finally lead to a second world war. But a group of philosophers meeting in Vienna in the thirties, and constituting the Vienna Circle, had started a movement of thought which has its still lingering effects in philosophy fifty or more years later. The group included Moritz Schlick, Rudolf Carnap, Otto Neurath. As an undergraduate I had been studying philosophy, with some emphasis on Plato and Aristotle. When I read these so-called logical positivists, I suffered an intellectual conversion. They seemed to me to be starting philosophy all over again in the clear light of a rational day, and outside the dusty, dark, and bookish rooms of the established professors. Like Descartes in the seventeenth century, they were making philosophy useful, and rejecting the self-protecting academic lumber inherited from the past, the relics of the Schoolmen.

Among the lumber inherited from the past, and still surviving among my teachers at Oxford, was the Hegelian tradition, by which I had been impressed as a schoolboy reading F. H. Bradley's *Appearance and Reality*. But Marxism, a comprehensive theory of human history, is itself part of the Hegelian lumber. According to the arguments first formed by the Vienna Circle, there cannot possibly be a comprehensive theory of human history, if only because no such theory is testable in experience, as all meaningful and acceptable theories must be. The new philosophers acknowledged the validity of mathematical knowledge in all its forms, and they accepted the theoretical and confirmed empirical claims of the experimental and observational sciences. They also accepted the narratives of historians in so far as they were strictly founded on cited evidence. But they rejected all metaphysical speculation, all moral and aesthetic theorising, all theology, all general theories of history, as not amounting to knowledge, even if some of them might have some value as rhetoric or as the expression of subjective feelings. Suddenly I was able to see all those political programmes which are founded on a theory of history as founded on a consoling illusion, whether it was Hegelianism, Marxism, Comtean positivism, or liberal doctrines of progress. Viewed in the light of the logical positivists' polemic, such presumptuous theories seemed simply the relics of the metaphysical systems which had succeeded the collapse of Christian faiths. They were secular versions of the story of Redemption, which would finally cause all the evils of history to disappear.

Outside mathematics, and in the real world of persons and objects, there is no secure knowledge that has not been tested in experience and that has not in this way been exposed to the risk of falsification. This was my belief at the time. Men of religion and, following them, the inventors of metaphysical systems needed to take a shortcut to their visions of the design of the universe, through revelation in sacred texts or through insight into alleged necessary truths. Real knowledge is always laboriously, and usually slowly, accumulated, piece by piece, experiment by experiment; and every advance opens up indefinitely extending areas of ignorance.

It therefore began to seem necessary that philosophy should finally abandon its shortcuts and its grandiose claims and should proceed in the tentative problem-solving style of the natural sciences. With this idea the study of the peculiarities of natural languages came to be considered a central part of philosophy. Then came the war, long anticipated. As an intelligence officer in the war for four years I studied the espionage and counter-espionage operations of the Reichssicherheitshauptamt, Himmler's Central Command, which controlled the whole of the SS, including the Gestapo, excluding only the Waffen SS. This experience altogether changed my attitude both to politics and to philosophy, as the full scale of the SS's operations in occupied Europe and in Russia became known, and as the programme announced in *Mein Kampf* could be studied in action. I interrogated some leading Nazis in captivity at the end of the war, including Heydrich's successor as head of the Reichssicherheitshauptamt, Kaltenbrunner, with whom I talked at length when he was a prisoner with U.S. Army headquarters, and whom I brought to London for further interrogation. I learnt how easy it had been to organise the vast enterprises of torture and of murder, and to enroll willing workers in this field, once all moral barriers had been removed by the authorities. Unmitigated evil and nastiness are as natural, it seemed, in educated human beings as generosity and sympathy: no more, and no less, natural, a fact that was obvious to Shakespeare but not previously evident to me. It became clear that high culture and good education are not significantly correlated with elementary moral decency. The massacres in the Soviet Union, continuing for decades after the war, fell into place alongside the work of Hitler and of the SS. They expressed a brutalised and debased Machiavellianism, the political style characteristic of the twentieth century. It seemed necessary to turn back to Machiavelli himself, looking over the heads, as it were, of the eighteenth-century moralists to the starting-point of modern secular thought about statecraft and morality.

There was a wonderful period of philosophical excitement in Britain, particularly at Oxford, after the war when the programme of step-by-step problem-solving was to a large extent realised in the movement called analytical philosophy, which took over some of the ideals of the Vienna Circle. It seemed that philosophical arguments could become more and more exact, scrupulous, and detailed, and the skills of philosophical argument were becoming more and more enjoyable. Even outside universities, and from the standpoint of general culture, both in the United States and Britain philosophical analysis, as a style of thought, was beginning to seem formidable, sometimes resented and sometimes praised: at least it was not just harmless, as academic philosophy had usually been in Britain. Some old problems of knowledge and of understanding were transformed by new kinds of argument within philosophy. These were the gentle post-war years, some of them with a Labour government, when Communism and anti-Communism were the preoccupations of Europe and of the United States, but not of Britain, where philosophy flourished within a stable liberal consensus. Marxism, the Communist Party, and the Catholic Church were the focusses of thought and of polemic which set the direction for Continental philosophies; but in Britain they were largely ignored. Analytical philosophers might happen to have political interests, but their philosophical arguments were largely neutral politically.

I did not return to the teaching of philosophy and to university life immediately the war ended. I remained in government service in a minor role until late in 1947, partly because the government was a Labour government. Almost everyone expected a period of Socialist and Communist dominance in Europe as a reaction to Nazism and to collaboration with Nazism. In the summer of 1947 I was involved in Paris in the preparation of the European response to the Marshall Plan. This is usually described as the turning of the tide in Europe, because widespread poverty and economic collapse were averted by the American action. I was impressed at that time, and I still am impressed, by this metaphor of the tide as applied to politics and to historical change. It fitted exactly the experience of the preceding five years. From all the dark years of Europe's history, two years, 1789 and 1917, had stood out in the light of my generation's attention, as if they alone were to set the recurring pattern of political development. We expected further social transformations, more years of revolution or near-revolution. But in fact tides come in, with accumulating appetites for improvement and liberation, and tides go out, with a tired call for peace and quiet and for security; and only an occasional flood tide disturbs this natural rhythm and inundates the land.

Not long after 1947 the pre-war Marxist illusions about history were called to my mind again when some friends who had also worked in secret intelligence during the war were shown to have been secret agents of the Soviet Union and I was interrogated about them and their motives. They had been dedicated to a cause, and the cause had its origin in a theory. The observed reality underlying the theory had been the gross inequalities in capitalist societies and the desperate poverty of large sections of the working class, poverty aggravated in 1931 by unemployment. A deep sense of injustice, a feeling of moral disgust, had been converted into an altogether different state of mind: a cool and apparently rational belief in a theory of history which had revealed the inevitable future. A sense of great injustice calls for action, and, deceived by theory, these British Communists had acted in support of an evil cause, overlooking the evidence of the Communist Party's mass murders, tyranny, and destruction. One could therefore ask why perceptions of injustice had to be disguised and deformed by philosophical theory before they were thought to be respectable.

The answer, I think, is to be found in a false epistemology then prevalent, and in a naive account of truth, which took the propositions of well-established scientific theories as the sole paradigm of literal truth. The prevailing, and often unspoken, philosophy of the liberal intelligentsia in Britain was still anchored in the dogmas of British empiricism, which entailed that an appeal to the notion of injustice as a ground for action must be merely the expression of subjective feeling. Moral propositions, unlike the propositions of natural science, of mathematics, and of ordinary observations of fact, are not to be taken seriously as either true or false.

I had been greatly interested in the processes of secret intelligence during the war. These always are processes of deception, intrigue, treachery, and mystification. The deception and intrigue sometimes go so far that any normal interest in literal truth is lost along the way, because the truth is buried beneath layer after layer of corrupt intention. Deception and concealment in politics, and the complexity of motive that leads to treachery, have always attracted me, both in reading history and occasionally in actual experience during the war. I have difficulty in imagining that purity of intention and undivided purposes can be the normal case in politics. I believe that very many people feel divided between openness and concealment, between innocence and experience; and, outside politics, they often find themselves divided between love and hatred of their own homes and of their own habits. The evidence for this belief of mine comes rather from fiction than from moral philosophy, which always presents a tidier picture in the interest of some prevailing epistemology. The evidence comes also from introspection; I am interested in deceit. These conflicts of feeling not only seem natural, they also are often useful. Enjoying the spectacle of duplicity and deceit in secret intelligence during the war, I did not doubt that there is a black hole of duplicity and intrigue into which the plans of politicians and intelligence officers may altogether disappear, because they may forget what they are supposed to be doing, lost in the intricacies of political manoeuvre. It is useful to understand the devious calculations which underlie the publicised features of international relations in war and peace; and one cannot easily understand such calculations unless one has at least some degree of sympathy with them, some fascination, however qualified, with the twists and turns of political contrivance.

Under contemporary conditions Machiavellian calculations immediately seem morally repellent, because of the risk to humanity as a whole if a serious miscalculation occurs. But it has not seemed to me sufficient, from a moral point of view, to dwell on the moral repulsion without at the same time exposing, as fairly as possible, the forces that drive governments to conceal the extent of the deceit and violence to which they hold themselves committed in defence of national independence. I have always been a Socialist, but in the thirties I hated the opposition to rearmament against Fascism which expressed the innocent hopes of some British Socialists. That policy seemed to me to identify morality with innocence, and this identification would ultimately set the politicians free to disregard morality altogether. I have always distrusted that element in British Socialism which might be called the vegetarian and pure-minded element. Observation of the politics of the immediate pre-war years first made me think about the unavoidable split in morality between the acclaimed virtues of innocence and the undeniable virtues of experience. Moral theory, trying for rational coherence, has covered over the rift and the tidier picture has become a kind of orthodoxy, even though it contradicts experience. This book is an attempt to bring the rift, and the consequent ambivalence, into full view, and at the same time to acknowledge that this purpose has its origins in a personal history as well as in philosophy.

It is natural to think first of the relation between gentleness and integrity, virtues in the private lives of persons, and the hardness and deceit that seem to be necessary in government and in the retention of power and effectiveness in public affairs: Machiavelli's problem. I had written briefly about this question in the composite volume *Public and Private Morality* (Cambridge University Press, 1978). I had hoped to draw attention to the superficiality, as I thought, of the current moral theories which bypassed Machiavelli's challenge. Most Anglo-American academic books and articles on moral philosophy have a fairy-tale quality, because the realities of politics, both contemporary and past politics, are absent from them. Yet Plato and Aristotle were surely right to think that virtues and vices in government, and in the uses of power, always constitute the greater part of morality, or at least one half of morality, when we come to reflect on our life and times.

The challenge is even more urgent than it was in Machiavelli's time, because much more than the independence of Italian city-states from foreign invaders is now at stake. A sufficient contempt for moral scruples in powerful governments, and an unclarity about the moral limits on violence, could possibly contribute to a universal, or at least to a very widespread, destruction of life in many parts of the world. Philosophical confusion, and general scepticism resulting from it, can lead to despair, to a sense that there is no solid ground to stand on when one is thinking of political conciliation and of the decencies of public life. Those who have power, and ordinary citizens and voters, may alike come to doubt whether there is any point in moral reflection where peace and war and government are concerned, if the reflection is easily subverted by philosophical scepticism about morality. Why start to think more carefully than the daily newspapers if philosophers have no clear notion of what constitutes the kind of careful thought which is relevant to public morality? It seems to me now that the problem which Machiavelli posed in unphilosophical terms, and in terms appropriate to his time, is a specification of a more general issue in moral philosophy, and, further, that this general issue, philosophical though it is, often does cause confusion, and does in fact lead to despair in day-to-day politics. The general issue is the incompatibility of different conceptions of the good life which are attached to different social roles and to the individual natures of very different human beings.

Machiavelli was not interested in philosophy either as it is now conceived or as it was conceived by Plato and Aristotle and by the Stoics. He did not intend to start a deep philosophical discussion about the nature of morality and of its authority. He was not particularly interested in scepticism, as applied to moral claims, in the style of the ancient sceptics. But by his concreteness and sharpness he forced the deeper question to the surface. Is there a clear distinction, even an opposition, between the negative and positive aspects of morality, that is, between morality as prohibition and limit, and morality as aspiration and ideal? Is there a perpetual, even a necessary, conflict in human nature between innocence and experience? Is there a foundation of public morality to be found in the indispensable institutions of political negotiation? Is there any reasonable answer to the historical relativist who claims that all conceptions of justice, including our own, reflect only a particular and transient way of life and have no validity, and no claim on us, outside their own particular setting?

These questions cannot be answered without provoking once again ancient doubts about the foundations of ethics and the nature of value judgments. Chapters 1 and 4 confront these doubts and propose some answers to them. In Chapter 4, "Hume's Ghost", I try by philosophical argument to change the dominant approach to the issues of moral scepticism and of the foundations of morality. I argue that moral judgments, and also our thoughts about moral issues, whether expressed or not, are best understood as a sub-class of judgments about possibilities, and that their natural setting is within deliberation, in public meetings or in silent thought, comparing and evaluating rival possibilities. Public deliberations take place in council rooms where the various interested parties meet and where their arguments for one policy or another are evaluated; this is the original Homeric setting of moral and political decision, when the council of leaders and heroes has to decide whether it is to be peace or war. There is a need for habits and for rules of procedure within this necessary institution, habits and rules guaranteeing that opposing viewpoints should be fairly heard and in due order assessed. From this predicament, encountered in almost any society, the core of a thin notion of minimum procedural justice is derivable, and the usefulness of this notion is elaborated in several chapters.

The philosophical point is that the moral concept, justice, is more clearly explained by reference to an actual type of human institution which is found everywhere, and not by reference to a proposition and a belief, or to a set of propositions and beliefs, which are supposed to be universally accepted, as social contract theories require. Similarly with the contrasting, and equally fundamental, moral notion of the good, and of conceptions of the good; this has to be referred back to the universal institutions and habits of praise and of admiration, and to our very diverse imaginations of how life might possibly be less mean and less disappointing. Men and women everywhere are always projecting new possibilities, either improvements to their actual way of life, or sometimes an altogether new way of life: not principally in response to their own immediate needs and desires, but rather in response to their conception of that which is admirable and untrivial in their lives. The particular possibilities which they envisage at any time depend upon their conceptions of the good at that time, that is, upon the activities and virtues which they believe constitute the best way of life within their reach.

Within philosophy one is apt to go astray, and to be caught in Hume's toils, because of a search for universally accepted propositions which should constitute the secure and indisputable ground on which all our moralising rests. The uses and forms of language, either in communication or in silent thought, arise from generally recurring types of situation which call for thought, and the diverse forms of language never become altogether independent of the typical social situations, and consequent inner reflections, which give rise to them: we cannot adequately explain to ourselves their sense and their implications without referring back to the recurring types of primitive situation. For example, when a person reflects, "If only I had kept quiet, the disaster would not have happened," the habitual emotion of regret which accompanies this reflection is as much a recurring and primitive feature of human behaviour as the emotion of hope for the future which is the natural background to the thought "If only I can keep quiet, all will go well." More of the situations would have to be revealed before the full sense and implications of the two judgments could be known, and before they could be evaluated as acceptable or unacceptable, true or false. One would need to know what background to the judgment was presupposed by the author, before one could determine more specifically what type of judgment was intended: for instance, whether it was a prudential or a moral judgment.

Moral reflections and moral judgments are of many different kinds, expressing not only regrets, hopes, and admirations, but also aspirations, condemnations, confessions, prescriptions, resolutions. Whatever the recurring type of situation in which they are imbedded, they always point to a contrast between the actualities and the possibilities: a contrast between the world as it is, or is likely to be, and what would have been better or worse, or what would in future be better or worse. At least since 1949 I have thought that the problem of singular hypothetical propositions ought to be the principal centre of interest for analytical philosophy, if only because judgments of this form are the meeting-point between theoretical and practical reasoning (see "Subjunctive Conditionals", reprinted in *Freedom of Mind and Other Essays,* Oxford University Press, 1971). In both contexts the conditions of their truth or acceptability cannot be determined without some knowledge of the presupposed background of the judgment. In this sense propositions about possibilities, past or future, are always problematic. They cannot be evaluated as true or false, acceptable or unacceptable, in isolation from a particular context in a particular type of discourse, which is marked by its own range of standard presuppositions. It is natural, but also inadequate, to think of a true proposition as typically corresponding to the world as it is, to an actuality; it is also natural to think that the correspondence should be directly visible or legible. Languages serve not only curiosity about the world as it is, but the whole range of human interests and emotions, including the emotions directed towards a better life, which exists only as an imagined, but perhaps real, possibility. This is the theme of Chapter 4, reversing the spectatorial conception of morality characteristic of Hume and of his intellectual heirs. There is a sense in which a judgment may be true in virtue of the real possibility which it indicates and describes: "If that bomb exploded here now, we would both be dead"—a judgment of fact, which may be true, and which is testable by observation of similar situations. Compare a moral judgment, which may be true also, and which is to be supported by some conceptions of the good: "If you deserted us now, that would be a betrayal and wrong."

I have hoped that the whole of my argument would be of interest to politicians and to laymen interested in politics as well as to philosophers, because it gives a coherent account, I believe, of the famous dichotomies that have haunted moral arguments and political philosophy: of reason versus emotion, of that which is eternal in morality versus that which is transient and dated. The aim is to persuade, and to change prevailing ideas about the way that arguments on moral issues must always proceed, in both public and private discussions. Simplified versions of Hume's moral scepticism have become almost an orthodoxy in English-speaking countries, and there is no method of proof which will correct them. Persuasion must take the form of reminding sceptical Humeans of the full range and variety of judgments and beliefs that play a part in their imaginations and deliberations about politics and personal relations. Perhaps they will then say: "Of course, there are these varieties: for instance, basic procedural justice as opposed to justice derived from a particular conception of the good—between unquestionable evils as opposed to evils that stand in the way of particular conceptions of the good. We do normally presuppose in our discussions that there are these differences and contrasts, but they are not usually picked out as necessary distinctions." That is the most agreement that an author could hope for in moral and political philosophy. Guided by different philosophical preconceptions, and by different moral concerns, other distinctions, also well founded, will at some time call for urgent attention as unreasonably neglected. Personal concerns of the author naturally make certain distinctions seem unduly neglected and particularly important. That is why I have traced this subjective element to its apparent sources in my experience, as clearly as I can.

In order to confront Machiavelli and Hume I must first consider Aristotle. Why Aristotle, so long ago and so remote from modern politics and from modern knowledge? Partly because of this remoteness, Aristotle had a clearer view of the reasonableness of practical reason and of the proper language of moral argument than any succeeding moral philosopher. I had originally argued in support of Aristotle's conception of moral and political judgment in an article published in 1949, on the grounds that Aristotle recognised that deliberation about practical possibilities ("What should I do?" "What is the right thing to do in these circumstances?") is the primary form of moral thought from which the primary form of moral judgment emerges: namely, the judgment that of all the possibilities that are open, the best action to take, all things considered, is so-and-so (see "Fallacies in Moral Philosophy", reprinted in *Freedom of Mind*). It has been a mistake of moral philosophers in the tradition of British empiricism to concentrate attention on the judgments that we make as criticisms of the behaviour of others, or on the comments that we may make on our own past conduct. This displacement of agency into observation can in part be explained by the dominance within modern Anglo-Saxon philosophy, particularly among those influenced by Hume, of an orthodox epistemology which takes scientific theory as the unavoidable standard, with the implication that all other types of theory, including moral theories, are approximations to it or weak imitations of it. We are then presented with the picture of the ideal moral observer searching in the world outside for the qualities and relations which correspond to our moral epithets "good" and "bad", "right" and "wrong". Not surprisingly, scepticism about the reality of moral distinction has been the effect of this picture, and the conclusion is reached that we paint things in the world either good or bad in accordance with the vagaries of our inner feelings. Aristotle knew nothing of scientific theory in its Newtonian and post-Newtonian shapes, and he was therefore free to describe the use of normative words in practical reasoning without assimilating them to an alien model. He kept a careful balance in describing the use of words in theoretical reasoning, which is directed towards a true description of external things and events, as opposed to practical reasoning, directed towards right choices in conduct: two different kinds of correctness, each in principle open to reasonable argument and counter-argument, and neither to be subordinated to the other.

In keeping this balance, Aristotle needed to argue against Plato's account of judgments attributing goodness to things. Plato had represented goodness as a common property imbedded in the structure of reality and open to our devoted study and contemplation. This theory left no sufficient place for the distinction between theoretical and practical reason, between thinking about actualities and thinking about possibilities; Aristotle therefore had to enter into the philosophy of language, upon which substantial issues of ethics depended then and still depend today. I must follow him into this philosophical grammar, even though he will be left behind after these preliminaries.

1

Parts of the Soul

❡ I have elsewhere argued that Aristotle gives the only comprehensive and correct account of the standard uses of the word
"good", and that he undermines equally not only Plato, but also
the various theories of the sense and uses of the word "good"
subsequently propounded by Hume, Mill, G. E. Moore, and by
the many platoons of emotivists and subjectivists and prescrip-
tivists in recent times (see "Ethics: A Defense of Aristotle", in
Freedom of Mind and Other Essays, Oxford University Press,
1971). Philosophical time and ingenuity have been wasted, because Aristotle, sympathetically interpreted, had already deline-
ated accurately the peculiarities of predications of good among
predications of other kinds. On the other hand the substantive
theory of the good, which he derived from his meta-ethics,
seems to me evidently and fatefully mistaken. Therefore I believe
that there is a mistaken step somewhere in the derivation. I believe I have identified that mistaken step.

I shall recapitulate as briefly as possible the doctrine about the
predication of good in the Nicomachean Ethics, stressing the
various steps downward that are important in inferring the human virtues and the nature and structure of the good for humanity. Against Plato Aristotle asserts that good is predicated in all
the categories, and that it is a mistake to think of goodness as

solely, or as essentially, a property or quality to be ascribed to various things: a quality like whiteness or yellowness. A good place to do something; a good time for something to happen; a good relation to have to someone or something: these are some examples of predications of good which are no less typical, and no less central and natural, than the use of the word "good" to evaluate a particular thing or a specific kind of thing. Plato was misled when he assumed that all predications of good must refer to a common quality and that they must be governed by a common criterion. The sense of the word is determined by a constant analogy which governs all its multifarious and disparate uses. If you want to attack the enemy, and I tell you that tomorrow at sunrise is a good time to attack, I give you necessary information, whatever my reasons may be, which ought to guide your choice of times, if I am right: analogously, I give you choice-guiding information when I tell you what is a good place, or the best place, to mount an attack. If anyone wants to attack, this is the very place for him or her to choose; it is top of the class of possible attacking points.

Extend this conditional wanting formula to attributive uses of "good" with common nouns which pick out a type or kind of object, whether artifact or natural object, describing it as a good so-and-so. One could begin with the examples associated with Platonic talk about the crafts and about artifacts, except that Aristotle is usually censured for choosing these untypical examples of predications of good and of representing them as typical: a "good knife", or the ambiguous "good food" (ambiguous between nourishment and taste), are instances. Critics of Aristotle claim that the implied notion translated as "function" is too narrow plausibly to cover this range of predications of good. But there is no reason to interpret this notion—what the type or kind typically or essentially does—so narrowly as to fit only straightforward cases of function. Consider the Aristotelian contexts: "good tragedy" and "good friend". In order to attach a determinate sense to these predications, we need to ask what a true or real or paradigmatic tragedy does for one, and hence to look for the grounds of classification which distinguish tragedies from, for example, melodramas and dramas of pathos. To ask what distinguishes a true or real friend from, for example, a boon companion is to ask what friends, as opposed to boon companions, characteristically do for one, and therefore what one wants a friend for. So one looks, in fact or in imagination, for the pure case of tragedy or friendship as opposed to the mixed cases, the central and complete specimens as opposed to the borderline or partial cases. If you want to see a real tragedy, or to find a real friend in a new place, and not just to find entertainment or a good companion, I will know what you want to find in the play and in the person, knowing what makes a tragedy a good tragedy and a friend a good friend, knowing what tragedies characteristically do for one, and what friends typically, and at their best, do. The paradigm of a tragedy—perhaps *Oedipus Rex*—produces all the effects which are essential to the recognition of a tragedy, and the ideal friends have all those effects on each others' lives which are essential to the discrimination of friendship among other human relations.

Not all classifications of natural kinds and types have as the grounds of classification the part that the kind plays in human life. Many scientific classifications are based on the genetic or morphological or other objective features of the kind or type. But pre-scientific classifications normally reflect the interest which the kind satisfies, or the part that the kind plays in persons' lives. This is evidently true when persons are classified under various headings: for example, as administrators or poets or businessmen or generals or fathers or citizens. These are classifications of human beings by human beings and, in virtue of their practical implications, they require that there should be some ordering of the desires and interests of the human beings referred to. X might have all the virtues essential to poets among other human functions, but none of the virtues of a father: ought X to allow his life to take this form? In other words, does being a good poet contribute more to being a good human being than being a good father? Aristotle argues that there must be an architectonic classification of human beings as such, as opposed to the classification of them in their roles as workers, friends, citizens, statesmen, poets, fathers. In this context the grounds of classification of human beings as human beings are not those that a systematic biologist uses, picking out observable physical and genetic features of the creature. Rather we ask the question: suppose we encounter some strange creatures from another planet, who are physically very unlike human beings as we know them; what features would be necessary and sufficient for us to regard them as human beings? Regarding them as human beings, in this context, implies also treating them as human.

At this point Aristotle, sympathetically interpreted, can make a philosophical virtue out of the apparent circularity of determining first what makes a good human being as a way to determine what makes a good friend, and then determining what makes a good friend as part of determining what makes a good human being. The moral ideal represented by a picture of a good human being would be utterly abstract, vague, and empty as a guide to action, if it had not been filled out by independently convincing pictures of the perfect friend, the good law-giver and statesman, the authentic thinker, the just member of the community, the good family man, and so forth. We may already have learnt in day-to-day experience what these several and separate human virtues and achievements are; but we turn to moral philosophy to learn "the reason why" these human virtues fit together in the style of conduct of a good human being. The virtues of human beings as such do not just form a list, not to be further rationalised; on the contrary there is an order of priority and subordination among them, and a principle, or central idea, determining the order of preference. The central idea is that a human being's distinction is to be able to think, and that we should regard the strange and apparently inhuman creatures as human if they proved to be capable of thought, and therefore of imposing general and explicit rules on their conduct and on their social arrangements and on their inquiries into reality. If we could have intelligent discussions with them about their policies, social arrangements, and beliefs, we should regard them as human beings for all practical purposes, even though they might be different from us in features that are of interest to physiologists and biologists.

The architectonic and ordering principle represents human beings as most human when they are most thoughtful and intelligent, both in practical activities and in theorising. Their characteristic and distinguishing virtues are all to be found in this area, in the intelligent control of natural feeling, for example, and in just and friendly dealings with other people. A person will have a satisfying life if and only if he realises in his activities all the essential potentialities of human beings at their best, with nothing wasted, no loss in a complete life. In one of my specialised roles, as philosopher or as politician, I may carry with me an ideal of the complete philosopher or the complete politician, but these ideals must find their place within the ideal of the complete human being. They are subordinate ideals, to be explained by the contributions which being a good philosopher and a good politician make to the exemplary human being.

At this point in his argument, and following a natural line of reasoning, Aristotle seems to me to go wrong. The requirement of perfection as a human being entails a complete life within which essential potentialities can be realised, and this in turn entails a principle of balance. There can be all-roundedness, an avoidance of eccentricity and lopsidedness, only if a person knows how to steer a middle path, and to avoid the inhumanity of the philosopher who has few human interests outside philosophy, or the inhumanity of the dedicated politician who has no time for friendship and for purely intellectual pursuits. Aristotle clings to something like the old Platonic ideal of justice as a balance of elements within the soul, as also in society: a cosmos to be discovered in the soul, as in the constitution of the physical universe. For Aristotle practical moral intelligence consists in finding a balanced diet for the soul, just as a balanced diet is required for the body—not too much dry food (research in libraries, perhaps) and certainly not too much sweet food (excessive attention to Italian opera).

My point of divergence is precisely this picture of the good person or good human being as necessarily being the perfect human being, rounded and balanced, necessarily not eccentric or lopsided, and the consequent representation of the good for man as to be attained only in the fulfilment of the standard and normal potentialities of human beings in a complete life. There seems to be no necessary connection between being an admirable human being and being a person who is the standard and normal and all-round and, in this sense, perfect human being. What has gone wrong? Where is the false step in Aristotle's argument? The notions of a good man and a good woman, and of a good human being, certainly make sense. Also it certainly makes sense to contrast the virtues that a person exhibits in a specific role, for example, as philosopher or poet or politician, with the virtues that he or she may have or lack as a human being. Why therefore cannot we follow Aristotle in claiming the architectonic and overarching role for the virtues of a human being as such?

Part of the answer is to be found in the notion of completeness and perfection. A good person, who is to be admired and praised, necessarily exhibits distinctively human characteristics to an exceptional degree. But he or she does not necessarily exhibit all or most of the distinctively human characteristics, nor are they always manifested in a balanced and a complete life. There certainly are predications of good in which the inference from a good so-and-so to a complete or perfect so-and-so is valid, particularly with natural kinds. But the entailment is not always in place, and particularly not with objects designed for human use. If I decided to give someone some very good china, the notions of completeness and of perfection are out of place, except in the sense that the china must not be broken or damaged, and in this minimal sense perfect: similarly for a good philosopher, good politician, good poet. They do not necessarily have to exhibit all the distinctive features of all good philosophy and all good poetry, or to have all the distinctive virtues of a politician. But they do need to be free of a minimal set of gross defects if they are to be praised under these headings. Over and above this minimum the poets and philosophers and politicians may be excellent in many different ways, exhibiting different sets of virtues, even if with some overlap, representing rather different ideals in poetry and philosophy and politics.

The same is true of the central, target-setting praise of human beings, and also of a human life, taken as a whole: the men or women praised, and picked out as examples, may have exhibited different ranges of human virtues above a certain minimum of necessary virtues which any praiseworthy person would be expected to possess. He or she could scarcely be said to have a good life, or be admired as a person, with no distinctive powers of mind of any kind, or no capacity for friendship or love, or no regard for fairness and justice in dealing with other people. But the proportion in which an admirable person may possess these virtues, or specific variants of them, may greatly vary. Correspondingly the specific moral ideals represented by different totally praiseworthy persons may be very different. A man or woman may be greatly admired, and may represent a moral ideal, because she dedicates her life to some single theoretical or artistic or practical aim, abandoning many normal human interests in pursuit of the aim, which is a benefit to mankind. Another person may be greatly admired, and may represent a moral ideal, because he has exhibited in his life, without any fame or glory, a disposition that causes him to be loved by a wide circle of friends and by his family, and to be a support of every institution with which he is in contact, and to be a model of incorruptibility and gentleness.

What then can be meant by *the* function or characteristic work (*Ergon*) of human beings, which supports the idea of human virtue, and of the supreme end for human life? If so much possible variety is admitted, can there be anything properly called the one all-inclusive end for man? Have we not returned by a roundabout route to the standard objection to Aristotle's deduction in Book

I of the Nicomachean Ethics, which uses the notion of the essence of humanity?

Reason and the Soul

❡ I shall argue that the principal mistake occurs not here, but one step later in Aristotle's argument, in his account of the human soul, and, more specifically, in his account of the distinguishing capacity to think. Let it be agreed that all living things have souls; we can even speak of vegetative souls and animal souls. These are the physical foundations of human behaviour which are appropriately studied in the biological sciences. But in a human soul the power of thought is superimposed on this limiting foundation. The power of thought is the source of the characteristic plasticity and diversity of human behaviour when compared with the behaviour of other animals. The essence of humanity, in the sense of the principal salient distinguishing characteristic, is precisely a perpetual openness to new ways of life, to new forms of thought, to innovations in language and in social arrangements. In comparison with other animals, human beings are born under-equipped for immediate survival, but with an extraordinary capacity to learn over many years by intelligent imitation. Within a common framework of species-wide needs and interests, they are ready to acquire the particular habits of speech and thought and behaviour which happen to prevail in their environment at the relevant time. Most of these habits of speech and thought and behaviour are very far from being species-wide. On the contrary they are highly specialised and divisive, marking and distinguishing one among a great variety of populations and of social groups.

Prominent among the essential potentialities of the human soul, of its distinctive function, is this capacity for linguistic, cultural, and moral diversity, for imaginative invention, which is to be ranked alongside the power of the intellect. The intellect unites humanity across all barriers and enables persons to communicate, in spite of their diverse languages, and to develop logic and mathematics and the natural sciences as a common possession. "Alongside" seems the appropriate word, because there is no good reason for exalting the power of intellectual understanding over the power of imaginative invention as being "the higher" power, or as more evidently distinctive of human beings. It is rather the contrast and tension between these two powers that is characteristic of the species.

A salient characteristic of human beings, distinguishing them from other living creatures, is their potentiality for many different specialisations of their abilities and interests, and consequently for many different ways of life which manifest these specialised abilities and interests. The human soul is not throughout structured into universally ordered potentialities dictating a definite and highly specific way of life for any creature within the species.

One must not exaggerate. Aristotle made the point that human beings are also biological systems, with the comparatively fixed and invariant capacities of biological systems, as well as the distinctively human learning capacities. I am arguing against the picture of the soul as vertically organised into three levels, higher and lower in the scale of being; and against the narrow specification of the distinctively human level under the heading of "reason", interpreted as Plato and Aristotle interpreted it. But I will not be disputing the Aristotelian claim that our notions of justice and of human worth, and of that which is admirable and desirable in human life, cannot be understood without some conception of a shared human nature as a set of shared potentialities. In addition, I claim that this conception is not arbitrarily asserted or assumed, but rather is tested by argument and by evidence of many different kinds. In agreement with Aristotle I shall argue that there are well-known conceptions of human potentialities which can be shown to be mistaken, including Aristotle's own conception: mistaken either because they are internally inconsistent, or because they are evidently incomplete in the light of evidence from history, personal experience, psychology, and anthropology.

The claim that many well-known assertions about human potentialities are mistaken and not reasonably defensible does not entail that we can hope to show that one, and only one, such claim is defensible and not mistaken. At this point I leave Aristotle because he believed that the essential human potentialities are fixed, once and for all, in a variety of senses of "fixed" in which I shall argue that they are not fixed. Any conception of human potentialities has to represent a target which is not only always moving, but also moving in several dimensions. Any single conception is either too abstract and too general, too lacking in complexity, to count as a representation useful for ethics; or the representation, faithful to the changing and moving target, is too evidently open-ended, and admittedly provisional, for any final truth to be claimed. The enterprise of the moralist, of which this essay is a specimen, ought to be the emendation and elaboration of those few well-argued conceptions of human powers which now actually influence people's lives and purposes. The inheritance from past speculation has established the vocabulary which one uses even while one tries to revise it. The attempt to correct past conceptions does not imply a belief in the finality of the suggested new version; it implies only a belief that the new version, in some sense, better represents the so far known features of human nature. The aim is to contribute to the inheritance.

Justice and the Soul

❧ Suppose that there is a contrast and a tension between the definite and shared human powers, traceable to species-wide needs, and the un-Aristotelian drive to diversity of human powers, traceable to individual needs. Always first among the shared human potentialities is the recognition of justice, which is necessary to all human associations: of the obligations of love and friendship and of families and kinships; of the duties of benevolence, or at least of restraints against harm and destruction of life.

All these duties and obligations, summarised under these headings, have their specific forms at different times and in different populations. But the common needs are recognisable through their diverse specific satisfactions. These needs, and the consequent potentialities and virtues, may be characterised as constituting the minimum common basis for a tolerable human life. They are in this respect comparable with the biological needs. They could be called the conditions of mere decency in human lives. Without some specific realisation of the virtues answering to these needs, human life becomes nasty and brutish, less than human.

From a philosophical standpoint the difficulty has always been to identify the common virtue of justice or fairness through the great variety of its different realisations. There may be, it is argued, a shared single concept of justice, but under this concept shelter a confusion of conflicting conceptions of this virtue. What is common and shared therefore leaves the duties and obligations, and the ways of life protected by them, entirely indeterminate and undecided. Consequently it is argued that there is not, and cannot be, a common conception of moral decency and of the necessary conditions of any tolerable way of life.

I cannot reply to this argument effectively until I have written about the other side of the tension pulling against the shared human nature: that is, the drive to radical diversity and individuality in persons and in human populations, and the needs associated with this drive. Why did Aristotle, writing about the distinctive features of human beings, not mention the Babel of natural languages, the proliferation of religions with their exclusive customs and prohibitions, the attachment of populations to their separate and peculiar histories, the manifold frontiers and barriers, with the aid of which social groups and populations try to maintain their separate identity? Why did he not see this species-wide divisiveness, the drive to separateness and conflicting identities, as at least one distinctive feature of human beings among all the animal species? I think there is an answer in a cause of blindness which is not peculiar to Aristotle. The same cause operates, though with somewhat different effects, in Mill and Kant, and it is built into our inheritance of moral thought.

The cause is to be found in the concept of reason and the presumed structure of the soul or mind which gives sense to this concept. Having only partially freed himself from Plato, Aristotle retains the model of the soul as corresponding to the due gradations of the social order: reason as the master and governing class, desire as properly the co-operative subordinate auxiliary class and our animal nature as a dumb proletariat. Society has its due subordinations and is fatally corrupted if they are reversed: so has the individual soul, equally corruptible, and justice as a virtue in the soul is the same as justice realised in a right relation between social classes.

It is important that this enduring model of the soul is a philosophical invention, with no contribution from any discipline outside philosophy. Philosophers have been free to construct models of the soul as they please to serve their moral and political advocacy. Philosophers advocating democracy rather than aristocracy can represent the soul as an assembly of conflicting desires, in which it is arranged that the strongest combination of desires will always come out on top and will determine action. For a democrat this is as it should be, with the state and the soul in harmony. Plato's and Aristotle's aristocratic models of the soul have no more, and no less, warrant than the democratic one. There is no independent reason why, after reflection, we should accept any one of them as a true representation of the human mind or soul. It is impossible to point to the decisive tests, or to the impartially collected evidence, on which a judgment as to the truth of these pictures could be based. The models are not to be assessed for correspondence with reality as an anatomist's chart, representing parts of the body, may be. The philosophical models can be ranked in respect of their pervasiveness, the degree to which they have passed as metaphors into the established idioms of ordinary speech. But this pervasiveness is no evidence of literal truth.

In fact, the leadership of reason, presumed to be a natural dominance; higher and lower levels in the soul, associated with this dominance; the focussing of reason on abstract truths of theory and on general principles—these features of the aristocratic model, coming from Plato and Aristotle, have become pervasive dead metaphors in the common European and American vocabulary. So also is the picture of the perpetual conflict of desires, the chaos among the unruly populace, which, like the mob in ancient Rome or in Renaissance Florence, needs to be mastered and controlled. The pictures now seem so natural, and as if unavoidable, that we do not recognise the historical contingencies from which they derive, and the place of old philosophy in first introducing the metaphors or quasi-metaphors. First comes the invention of the distinct faculties with their proper limits; second, their hierarchical arrangement from high to low, from master to slave. These two elements in the aristocratic picture of the soul are not unavoidable nor are they in any other sense necessary. They are neither imposed upon us by observation of the operations of our mind, nor are they deduced from any first principles. The picture has gained acceptance and survived because it has so conveniently matched the prevailing social structure, and the justificatory ideologies, of European societies up to the present time. Even when Hume inverts the hierarchy, and claims that reason both is and ought always to be the slave of the passions, he naturally uses the old slave and master metaphor. A hierarchy remains in place, even if the aristocratic class, generally recognised as such, has been so narrowly restricted in its functions that it has become effectively powerless.

All pictures or models of the human mind and of its faculties, whether Aristotle's or Hobbes's or Spinoza's or Hume's or Kant's or Freud's, are inventions for a philosophical and moral purpose, and they are all in this sense arbitrary. In the sense that we are compelled to distinguish our arms from our legs, and both from our trunks, these distinctions of parts of the body, with their associated powers of movement, are certainly not arbitrary. There may be some degree of looseness, even of arbitrariness, in distinguishing their functions, but not in specifying their typical movements and their operational relations to each other. These relations and causal dependencies are strictly observable and test-able. But the operations of parts of the mind are shadowy enti-ties, and so are their relations to each other, because the mind, unlike the brain, does not literally have identifiable parts. We cannot in a class-room hang on the wall a chart that shows the parts of the mind and their mutual dependencies, and then claim that this presents the current state of agreed scientific knowledge about the mind's workings; and this inability is not to be ex-plained in the same way as our present inability to exhibit in any fine detail the workings of the brain.

Some of the gross operations of the brain, and their localisa-tion, can in fact be represented on a chart as accepted knowledge in physiology. Progress in understanding the operations of the brain, and in determining its fine structure, has been slow; but there is no *a priori* reason to doubt that progress will continue and that it will accelerate in time with a general advance in the physical sciences. We do not even know with any clarity what we would mean by agreed scientific knowledge of the operative parts of the mind, except in so far as such knowledge is derivable from knowledge of the operations of the brain. We can learn that chemical and surgical interventions in certain regions of the brain will have very specific effects on specific mental operations. This advancing knowledge might enable us gradually to attribute parts to the mind corresponding to the distinct operating parts of the brain: at least we should be able to do this if naturally and independently distinguishable functions of the mind proved to be conveniently localised in distinct areas of the brain. Then the parts of the mind would be the distinct shadows of distinct parts of the brain. But it is not likely that this structural correspon-dence will be discovered, if only because mental operations have hitherto been distinguished and identified by a set of criteria which are unconnected with the operations of the brain.

I do not deny that there is some rough objectivity in most of the distinctions between different types of mental operation which we ordinarily make, and therefore in the derived distinctions between mental faculties. We know sufficiently what we mean when we distinguish between the performances of a person's intellect, memory, powers of observation, imagination: sufficiently, that is, for ordinary, rough-and-ready purposes in social transactions and in conversation. The power of argument and of calculation on one side, and the power of memory on the other, are famously distinct in persons, and they are also clearly linked to distinct types of theoretical inquiry and to distinct virtues in practical affairs. There is so far no error or unclarity in talking metaphorically of reason and memory, alongside powers of perception, as faculties in the soul. But as soon as someone needs to know, for some serious purpose, what is the range of reason, and what is to be counted as argument or calculation or reason, indeterminacy and unclarity begin. Is the careful thought that a sculptor gives to the precise modelling or carving of a figure to be counted as calculation, and as an exercise of the intellect? Is the utterance of a correct sentence, not previously heard, in a foreign language to be counted as a feat of memory, rather than as some unconscious conditioning or as some aspect of habit? If such questions as these are pressed, no clear answer can be found in ordinary usage and at a pre-theoretical level. At least it becomes necessary to state the purpose for which the more exact demarcations are needed. Even then no definite and secure answer may be forthcoming, until we have more knowledge of the determining mechanisms in the brain.

The hierarchy of faculties in the soul, with reason as the appropriate governing class and desires as the restless proletariat, remains a familiar picture through Aquinas and into the eighteenth century. The desires do all the real, rough work, moving us to action, but they ought to be both dominated and penetrated by reason as the policy-maker. Subordination and consequent stability in the state: subordination and stability in the soul. There cannot be collaboration among the social classes, each recognising its due place, unless it is acknowledged that virtue in the soul is also a habit of obedience, and is the acknowledgment of the proper dominance of the higher over the lower, the abstract and spiritual over the concrete and material. Practical reason is to be modelled on the deliberations of the chiefs in the council chamber, providing the arguments for and against, and the populace of contrary desires must be brought into line with the conclusion. By themselves the proletarians would never agree on a plan and adhere to it. The people is an anarchy of compelling appetites, all on the same level. This is the Hogarthean image.

The Aristotelian picture of parts of the soul and of practical reason is an ideology so deeply entrenched both in philosophical ethics and in ordinary language that perhaps it is impossible to unravel the metaphors of obedience and of social conflict which run through conventional talk about the mind or soul and its virtues. It may be argued that the language which describes mental processes must unavoidably be transferred from the description of public transactions, because the public transactions are a common point of reference and inner processes have to be modelled on them. But even if this is true, we do not have to accept the normative implications of the ideology of higher and lower faculties, and of the virtues connected with the obedience of the lower. One can go behind the ideology and look at the facts.

Thought and Reflection

❦ What are the facts in this context of moral speculation? First, they are the facts of history, which record the different types of thoughtful activity which have been picked out as conspicuously valuable and praiseworthy in different times and in different places, and the reasons given for the admiration and praise. In any context that borders on philosophy, the term "reason" is incurably tainted by its ideological and normative connotations. The word "thought" is comparatively innocent and colourless, and not confined to particular methodologies and particular domains. A thoughtful activity is any activity in which the agent is to some degree controlled by a standard of correctness and of mistake. Every game or sport or craft or art involves thoughtful activities, and obviously all scientific and professional and political activities involve thought. We need not so far be committed to any comparative evaluations and ranking of the thought in the different domains. We need not, for instance, rank them on a scale as approximations to pure thought at the top of the scale, pure thought being the most abstract thinking, the most supra-mundane and God-like. Perhaps arguments can be developed for regarding thoughtful activity in one or other of these domains as intrinsically superior, and there may be arguments for constructing an order of priority among them. But these must be arguments, and not merely the implications drawn from the traditional connotations of the word "reason".

But is the concept of thought, not further restricted, too neutral and too empty to enter usefully into any argument about human values and about good and evil? It is not. The concept of thought, fully secularised and separated from God, does not become so general as to be without content. An activity has become unthinking or thoughtless when we have neglected to apply any standard of rightness and mistake to the performance, when we have just gone ahead without reflection and control. In general it is reasonably assumed that thoughtlessness in the performance of any valued activity is a recipe for failure. Reflection and control are the necessary notions that constitute thought across all the domains of thoughtful activity; and "reflection" is a word that can be used to represent a distinct phenomenon in conscious experience. We unavoidably know the difference in experience between the thoughts that from time to time occur to us and the line of thought that we pursue while we are concentrating on some thought-controlled activity. This is the familiar distinction between activity and passivity of mind, to which many philosophers have referred but which no one, I think, has succeeded in analysing. The distinction, with a scale from active to passive thinking, is an incontestable phenomenon, and it is not an invention of philosophical theory: there is the felt difference between doing something with care and attention and doing it while thinking of something else, or the difference between concentrating on a problem and its possible solutions and just drifting and allowing one's thoughts to stray. Every schoolmaster and instructor knows the imperative: "Just think and you will find the answer." Everyone knows from experience the occasions on which, while one is exercising a skill, one's thought strays or is distracted, and one is no longer directing thought to the task in hand.

This phenomenon of active and directed thought also presents itself in consciousness as a phenomenon of ownership and self-assertion. The thoughtful self is the supervisory self which keeps watch over the performance in hand with a view to avoiding mistakes. These phenomena of consciousness, reflected in idioms of speech, give a clear sense to the overlordship of thought in the soul and to its exaltation above other faculties of the soul, such as feelings of pleasure or tiredness, of satisfaction or of dullness. The metaphor of height seems entirely appropriate, even inevitable. Supervising is looking down, and while we are thinking, we have the power to withdraw further in order to supervise our present thinking processes. As we do so, we seem to assert ourselves and to exercise our power of thought. We seem not to allow our thought to drift onwards as the immediate effect of external causes and of the association of ideas. There certainly is a pre-theoretical sense in which we may intelligibly speak of the natural dominance of thought within the soul or mind, of its exaltation to a higher level than the functions of the mind which it surveys and corrects. The dominance can be called natural, because no one will want to dispense with the governance of thought in his skilled activities, unless perhaps in the interest of spontaneity and of naturalness in special cases.

To admit this natural dominance is to admit only one comparatively small part of Aristotle's account of reason's dominance. First, I am discussing thought, not reason, and thought is a much more general and less specific term. Thought, unlike reason, is not restricted in the domain of its operation: reason is restricted to argumentative domains, in mathematics, logic, natural science, and law. Thought operates in any domain of activity to which success versus failure, or correct versus incorrect, applies. Second, the dominance of thought as the supervisor of other activities does not involve any metaphysical distinction between a faculty of pure thought, which is a God-like activity, and lower, because impure and mixed, forms of thought. There is nothing in the concept of thought, the governing faculty, which entails that thought about thought is higher and more God-like than thought about an activity which is not thought. No scale of value between higher and lower domains of thought is implied by the conception of thought as reflection and supervision. The only normative implications come from the distinction between active and passive thought. The obvious normative implication is that a person actively directing his or her thought is an autonomous agent, fully responsible for what he or she achieves, and in this respect to be praised.

So far we have no reason to single out domains of thought as being more admirable and more desirable in virtue of being more pure and therefore more God-like, or as being less concerned with perception and the senses, or as being directed towards abstract generalities rather than to concrete individuals. So far we do not have a reason to consider theoretical reason, concerned with truth, superior to practical reason, concerned with the arts of government, or to admire tragedy more or less than comedy. If we must find grounds for such comparative evaluation, because we need to make choices, the grounds must not be squeezed out of the bare concept of a thinking animal.

Reason and Imagination

❡ Recognition of the reflective and supervisory nature of all thinking, of the "stepping back" process, leaves most normative questions open, to be decided on grounds that are independent of Aristotle's metaphysics. Is there anything that compels us to value the study of mathematics more highly than the study of history, or to value logic more highly than sculpture, or to prize and encourage scholarship more or less than natural science? There is one distinction. The kind of thought which in the past has been distinguished as reason directs those inquiries which are not confined by the notations employed in them to any specific culture, nor tied to any particular natural language. The thinking contained in purely intellectual activities crosses all frontiers; the thought is not of its nature best expressed in one language rather than in others. The thought is designed to be universal in the sense of ecumenical. The word "reason" has in its history been used to mark that element in human thought which is common to all thinking individuals. Theorems in mathematics, and their supporting proofs, and arithmetical calculations, are immediately accessible to everyone everywhere, whatever language they speak, sometimes with a relatively trivial call for translation. It has been generally recognised that to learn mathematics is to learn the clearest methods of reasoning.

There is another and easily distinguishable kind of learning, which begins in early childhood, and to which human beings seem pre-adapted by mechanisms that are so far not understood: this is learning to understand and to speak one's own language. The stress here is on the possessive "one's own". Learning one's own language is precisely and conspicuously to acquire a power that separates one's own people from the great mass of mankind with whom one cannot immediately and easily communicate, unless it be at the chess-board or in some mathematical notation. This is an intimate, normally unforced and largely unregulated, learning, in which mimicry and pre-conscious memory play a predominant part, and which is certainly not thought of as a manifestation of reason. Following the adults to whom she listens and whom she imitates, the child needs to store in her mind the idioms of grammar and of vocabulary peculiar to this first language. Usually it is difficult to give a logically compelling reason why the idioms are as they are, and usually the most plausible explanation is to be found in some accident of history. It is a domain in which most of the idiosyncrasies of the language which have to be learnt present themselves as arbitrary and conventional. They are contingent facts which have to be remembered, in the same way that individual places and names of persons have to be remembered. The learning is a process of familiarisation, of acceptance of the way one's own world works, as one at first accepts the persons who constitute one's own family and the house that happens to be one's home. One tries to learn to be at ease in one's own language exactly as one tries to be at ease with one's own people and to imitate and to follow their customs and observances. This happens while it is naturally, if gradually, realised that one's own family, one's own home, and one's own language exist alongside uncounted millions of other families, homes, and languages; homes, families, and languages from which one has been cut off in a process of familiarisation which is a process of seclusion. Natural languages, unlike the products of reason, serve the purpose of setting up frontiers between populations and of dividing humanity into uncommunicating fragments. The other side of this coin is the more often emphasised fact that a natural language is one of the three most powerful bonds that make a population a salient and self-conscious unity. The other bonds that famously convert a population into a community are a shared locality and a shared history of victories and defeats. Language has proved itself in history to be the equal in strength of the other two as a force for unity.

The powers of mind that enter into the mastery of a natural language, whether it is a first language or not, have to be characterised in a way that sets them apart from the mastery of some symbolic system or of some purely rational structure of thought. Memory, and particularly pre-conscious memory, is certainly one power; the gift for imitation, which can develop into the art of parody, is another. In addition there is an emotional factor which it is impossible to analyse and difficult to describe. A normal person feels himself to be so closely enclosed in his own language that his relations with other people and with the external world are wrapped up in this local dialect.

Language and Knowledge

❡ If we were to encounter strange humanoid creatures who seemed to lack the capacity to follow an elementary argument, or to make elementary inferences, we should have reason to doubt their humanity. If these creatures lacked a natural language, which they had inherited and learnt, we should also have a reason to question their humanity. If they are to deserve the title of being fully human, it is not enough that they are ready to infer that if today is the first day of the week, then tomorrow is the second. We should also expect them to want to tell each other stories, and to be interested in recalling their own past and parentage. If they lacked these dispositions and powers, but at the same time were excellent reasoners, we should think of them as very superior robotics, an Alan Turing who had preserved no link with his schooldays at Sherborne, or a John von Neumann who had never reflected on his school in Budapest. Persons who conspicuously enjoy and excel in reasoning, but who have no interest in any kind of story-telling or in recalling and recording their past, tend to be considered monsters of rationality, and to be called inhuman. The truth is that one half of their humanity is missing, and that is the half which is least likely to be duplicated, or effectively simulated, by any machine, by any imagined non-corporeal being, or by any animal. Enjoyment of a historical language, which is one's own and which is certainly not a species-wide instrument of thought, is distinctively human. Particularly because any natural language differentiates the population using it from the great mass of the species, it helps the individual to establish his own identity as being different from the great mass of humankind. All humanity is, or can be, united in responding to Euclid's demonstrations; humanity is irreparably and forever divided in responding to Racine and to Jane Austen.

There is no one word, and no one concept, corresponding to the concept of reason, which has been used to represent the powers of mind involved both in the mastery of a native language and in translation from one language to another. There is no concept that stands in the same relation to linguistic skills which the concept of reason has to skills in logic, mathematics, and valid inference generally. No distinct part of the soul has been allotted by philosophical theory to the mastery of languages. A relevant philosophy here is that of Vico, whose "New Science" of philology, as he conceived it, was the historical study of human nature, and of human knowledge, largely through the development of language in individual minds and in history. This historical study of human nature and knowledge was designed to replace the dominant Cartesian study of human knowledge by inquiry into the rational foundations of knowledge, foundations that do not come to be and pass away, as the forms of language do. Vico's philology embraced what we would call social anthropology, the history of literature and of art, the study of myths, the study of grammars and vocabularies and their development, the history of legal systems and of the concept of law, and the history of literature. In short, philology embraced the whole of the humanities, as conceived in a contemporary university; and Vico argued against Descartes that these historical studies could provide a greater certainty than is possible in the natural sciences.

Vico's theory of knowledge takes historical knowledge as the paradigm of secure knowledge rather than mathematics and the natural sciences. Vico's principle of ranking is the *verum factum* principle: truth resides in what we have made. God made the natural world, and he possesses the certain truth about it, but we do not and will not. Human beings made their own history and their own cultures, and they can recapture, and represent to themselves, exactly what they made. In developing this epistemology, Vico puts alongside the faculty of intellect the faculty of imagination, which Descartes and Spinoza had made the typical source of illusion and error. Vico exalted the faculty of imagination as the creative aspect of the human mind, which generates new forms of language, new images and metaphors, and new cultures, while the intellect, the power to put thought in a tidy order, is the fading coal which survives in periods when the creative imagination has sunk low. The development of the mind begins with poetry, with the great fictions of Homer's epic and of classical drama, and it matures into the cool, analytical prose of Cartesian philosophy, so thin and inert in content that the mind finally has to renew itself once again with a revival of poetic imagination, with fiction and with myth. He turns the Aristotelian and Cartesian estimation of parts of the soul upside down, and puts the figurative, concrete, poetical, synthetic power of imagination on top as the directing power of the mind and as the most valuable, with the intellectual, abstract, prosaic, and analytical power as subordinate and derivative. We need to recapture the fantasies and wildness of childhood imagination and of the early world, before the ages of literal veracity, if civilisation is to renew itself before it thins out into a dry rationalism.

One can remain neutral in this dispute about dominance and subordination, and still take from Vico the suggestion that the imagination should be designated the power that is used when literary, linguistic, and historical skills are in play: just as reason is the power employed when argumentative, logical, mathematical, and calculative skills are in play. So far we have them on the same level, neither subordinated to the other. Considered as parts of the soul, both powers have to be both employed and educated as persons come to maturity, in any culture which is to survive. But there is a doubt about the unity, or coherence, of the interests that are to fall under the heading of imagination. With some cost in precision one can group together as imagination all serious and intense thinking which is not primarily concerned with arguments and with consistency, but rather with concrete representations of reality in some medium or other, including language, and also with fictions of many kinds. We probably do better, for most purposes, to think of reason and imagination as

entering into different thoughtful activities in different propor-
tions, rather than as determining distinct domains.

For Kant, and for utilitarians of all kinds, and for many generations of deontologists, practical reason ought to be the dominant power in the soul, controlling and directing emotions and
desires. These theorists do not recognise any large and distinct
place for serious, but non-argumentative, thought in the direction of a person's life, serious thought that could be called imaginative in the sense suggested. Some of these theorists allow a
large place for emotions and desires, in due subordination, in
determining the conduct of a person's life; but not for the kind
of reflective thought which is not primarily argumentative and
which is not primarily concerned with rules, principles, or other
generalities. This is the kind of thought that issues in the ability
to choose the right word in a translation of a poem from one
language to another, or to choose the right words to convey the
quality of a person who has recently died, when the words will
matter. It is the kind of thought which good actors undertake in
the course of deciding in detail how to play their parts, or painters or pianists as they pause to review their work. It is the kind
of thought which a historian gives to representing, on the basis
of the evidence, the combination of motives that led the statesman to take his fateful decision.

Suppose the concept of imagination is made to sweep over the
whole immense area of serious, non-argumentative thought: we
do not need to assimilate the judgments and beliefs which issue
from the imagination in this philosophical sense to the special
sub-class of pure aesthetic judgments, as characterised by Kant
in the *Critique of Judgment*. These have additional peculiarities as
judgments about the beautiful and the sublime in art and in nature. Later the Romantic movement, both in Germany and in
England, caused the imagination to be linked specifically with
aesthetic experience and artistic genius. There is a philosophical
point to be made in widely extending the range of the concept
from this narrow base. Aesthetic experience and artistic genius,

as they are characterised by Kant, can be represented as the splendid top of the vast iceberg of non-argumentative thought, most of which is submerged and does not attract any special attention. Logic, mathematics, and the theory of statistics and probability can be thought of as the top of the iceberg of argumentative thinking, all of which is subject to canons of rationality and of good order. The ensuing chapters must show the separate and complementary parts that the two powers of mind play in the conduct of a person's life.

2

Justice and History

⁋ Let it be accepted that we have to borrow the vocabulary that is to describe the operations of our minds from the vocabulary that describes the public and observable transactions of social life. The picture of the mind that gives substance to the notion of practical reason is a picture of a council chamber, in which the agent's contrary interests are represented around the table, each speaking for itself. The chairman, who represents the will, weighs the arguments and the intensity of the feeling conveyed by the arguments, and then issues an order to be acted on. The order is a decision and an intention, to be followed by its execution. This policy is the outcome of the debate in the council chamber.

Practical Reasoning

⁋ This model of practical reason as deliberation, surviving from Aristotle until the present day, is still as vivid and plausible as ever. There are good reasons for the survival, and for the apparent indispensability, of the model. Wherever and whenever human societies exist, whether they are primitive or technologically advanced, issues of policy will be debated in some assembly of chosen persons, whether a democratically or aristocratically chosen assembly, or an assembly chosen simply by monarch or tyrant. The institution of articulating and reviewing contrary opinions on policy is of necessity species-wide. The deliberations of the council of war in the *Iliad* are parallelled by the inner discussion preceding action within the soul of any prudent man. The parallel is not an accident: it is the parallel between a shadow, the inner process, and what it is a shadow of, the public institution. A substantial and manifest transaction takes place in the council of war, with identifiable and named persons entering the discussion in a definite sequence. This is an observable reality, while the single agent's inner debate is a metaphorical debate. The prudent person silently marshals and reviews arguments for and against alternative policies, and perhaps sometimes the arguments occur to him in some still identifiable and definite order, one after another. But it need not be so, even with the most clear-thinking person, and often the arguments present themselves in no definitely assignable order. We do not expect the model of deliberation, derived from discussion in the council chamber, to be reproduced with unquestionable literalness in the inner forum, any more than we expect our mental arithmetic to reproduce step-by-step the successive moves of a calculating machine.

There is an important difference between taking public debate as the model of the operation of the mind in practical reason and taking the visible operations of a machine as the model of the mind in arithmetical calculation. The rightness or wrongness of the outcome of an arithmetical calculation is quite independent of the moves made in arriving at the conclusion. Different people might reach the same true conclusion in two steps or in twenty. The practical conclusion of a debate on policy, whether in public or in the mind, is not similarly independent of the particular arguments which have led to the conclusion. The arguments that have led to the conclusion may be entered into the full characterisation of the conclusion itself. The outcome is often a decision to perform certain actions for certain reasons, and the moral quality of the decision in part depends on the acceptability of the reasons: are they a sufficient justification of the action? Therefore practical reasoning requires explicit formulation of reasons as a defence of the policy adopted. There is a call for articulateness and for distinct specification of the arguments for and against alternative policies, if the decision is to be understood and evaluated.

Uniting all humanity, from the nursery to the grave, the practice of promoting and accepting arguments for and against a proposal is taken as the core of practical rationality. The procedure is as well recognised and respected as the procedure of counting, and as unavoidable. It is of the essence of the procedure that the pro and the contra should both be heard and evaluated, and that the procedure should not be cut off before all the arguments are in. The discussion of an issue of practical policy is both an adversary procedure, with two sides represented, and a judicial one, because in the end a Solomonic judgment will normally be made, with the acceptance of some arguments and the dismissal of others.

The canons of rationality are here the canons of fairness. If the full procedure of discussion, and the weighing of arguments, has not been followed, the final judgment is tainted with bias and unfairness, even if, considered in abstraction, it seems to be fair, and seems to be the judgment that probably would have been reached if there had been full and fair argument. The notion of rationality in practical issues, as Aristotle knew, does not allow the evaluation of the reasons for a decision to be cleanly separated from the evaluation of the decision itself. Justice and fairness, at their most abstract level, are specifications of the notion of practical rationality, that is, of decision-making in difficult cases. Therefore justice and fairness are always in part procedural notions; a decision, whether in a law court or by a deliberating person in private, can be accepted as completely just and fair only if the reasoning that supports it has been adequate, and the main relevant considerations have in fact been impartially weighed in the balance.

There is an ambiguity here in the phrase "the reasoning that supports it", an ambiguity often stressed. The phrase could refer to the reasoning of the deciding agent at the time, or it could refer to the arguments that might be produced by anyone in a justification of the decision; and there are other possible interpretations, for example, the phrase could refer to retrospective justification of the decision by the agent. These meanings are different, and the differences between them certainly affect the evaluations of the person and of the policy adopted. But they leave intact the point that the decision can normally be characterised as fair and reasonable only if the supporting procedure and process can be characterised as fair and reasonable.

Procedural Justice and Historical Possibility

❡ The procedures of adjudication, which require the weighing of arguments, are in fact understood and applied across many varieties of barriers: across the frontiers of religious belief, across national loyalties, across philosophical and moral barriers. They are employed, and have been employed throughout history, between hostile powers in negotiation. This ought not be found surprising, precisely because the methods of adjudication and arbitration and negotiation are the outward equivalents of the methods of thought that everyone employs to some extent, and in proportion to his or her rationality, in inner debates. Two representatives of competing social groups, seated across the table in negotiation and with an arbitrator at the head of the table, are driven by the situation to produce arguments and rebuttals that can be weighed and pondered. Often the very physical setting itself, with an equal number of delegates on each side of the table, expresses the norm of fairness which is to govern the negotiation. Similarly, two competing interests of mine, which are making incompatible demands upon me and disrupting my life, need to have their claims weighed as fairly and reasonably as possible.

One must first remember the virtually inexhaustible variety of social conditions in which the rational procedures of adjudication and policy-making are observed. The different conflicting claims which are weighed in the same society at different times in its history, and in different societies all over the world, form an utterly heterogeneous set. Nothing unifies the set except, first, the necessity of preventing the conflict of interests from becoming a physical conflict—the Hobbesian "war of all against all"; and second, the consequent necessity that the method of adjudication should be known, understood, and generally respected in actual practice. No substantial principles of justice are so far implied by the existence of a procedure of weighing, and of adjudicating between, competing claims. The concept of justice preserves its sense through a variegated history, because of the distinct function that justice has in any society, and because of the rough similarities between the institutions and procedures which help to fulfil this function. It is universally true that where kinship and friendship fall short, justice in some acknowledged form has to step in, if conflicts are not normally to be resolved by force.

Particular conceptions of justice noted by historians and by social anthropologists have largely been formed by the same diverse imaginations that have formed different languages, different family structures, different social classes, different social myths, different religions and different moralities dependent on them. I write "largely", because the elementary procedural concept of justice, a constant in human affairs, interacts with varying particular conceptions of justice. For example, in a hierarchical society, where the ruling classes are allotted distinct roles by the accepted social myth and by religious doctrines, there will still be a place for procedural or quasi-procedural arguments about fairness in allocation of rewards and penalties, and these arguments may undermine the independently accepted ideas of social differences. This tension has been in fact a constant engine of change in Western societies. The monarch, for example, in some centuries has evoked continuing loyalty and awe, but arbitration between competing interests in society has gradually introduced, through the very process of arbitration, modified conceptions of fairness and justice, which in time have undermined the monarch's powers. Or again, the myths of early capitalism made factory legislation seem a harmful abuse of state power, an intrusion into the inviolable liberties of the capitalist. But the early organisations of workers submitted claims in the name of elementary justice, and then poverty itself became a two-sided and argued issue of social justice. The "condition of the people" question had been added to the agenda for adversary arguments between the moral reformers and the defenders of the status quo, who were brandishing a specific morality of free enterprise. Is it really unjust to restrict the property rights of factory owners?

The same pattern can be seen in recent years in the movement for women's rights and feminist causes. As with challenges to the divine rights of the monarchy or to the liberties of the investor, so with the rights of women there were precursors who attacked the prevailing social myth long before social changes, accelerated by wars, made the myth about the sexes more and more difficult to defend and lent the challenge to it some political force. This same pattern is repeated in the history of the abolition of slavery in the last century. First come the precursors, the "premature" advocates of a cause which will finally seem to most people obviously just, but which at first seems a denial of the natural and divine order of things, not open to practical reasoning; then comes the formation of pressure groups which represent some powerful interests in the society, usually, but not always, material interests; third, within the institutions of the state, democratic or otherwise, arguments for and against slavery have to be weighed and adjudicated within prevailing, but also changing, conceptions of justice.

Once a question about the injustice of slavery has been raised, and raised with political clout behind the question, the conception of justice which has supported the institution of slavery is already beginning to change. That conception depended on thinking of slavery as part of the natural order of things, to which no man-made alternative can usefully be imagined; it had placed slavery outside the sphere of practical reasoning, just as the authority of the monarch, or the free market for industrial products, or the subordination of women, were all in their time outside the sphere of practical reason—they were parts of the natural order. As Aristotle insisted, we do not deliberate about things that we believe cannot in the nature of things be other-wise. The function of social myth has always been to restrict the area in which practical reasoning can operate for human im-provement, by representing the particular social arrangements of particular societies as unalterable parts of the natural or divine order of things. Practical reason becomes innovative in human affairs when it demands reasons for practices which have been so represented, such as poverty or the subordination of women. In previous ages of which we have record the fallacy of false fixity, as it may be called, is almost always at work, disguising the in-justices attached to particular ways of life. It should now be pos-sible to assess the particular costs in injustice of present ways of life and present conceptions of the good from a comparative point of view and without self-protecting blinkers. That animals have no souls and therefore no feelings that demand respect; that primitive societies are always by nature morally inferior to advanced and civilised societies; that variations on a single pattern of sexual intercourse are unnatural perversions—these are a few of the false fixities designed to protect particular ways of life.

That an absolute monarchy leads to injustices; that it is unfair and exploitative to exact a day of ten hours' labour in filthy con-ditions from factory workers; that slavery is a grossly unjust in-stitution; that it is unfair that women should not receive equal pay for equal work—these are all propositions involving the con-cept of justice which most people in the 1980s will confidently assert to be true. There have been long periods in the past when reasonable persons would not have been confident about them, and would not have endorsed them as certainly acceptable. Nei-ther monarchy, nor factory labour and its conditions, nor slav-ery, nor women's rights were considered matters up for rational judgment as either just or unjust. Substantial, non-procedural conceptions of justice were embedded in ways of life, each with its distinctive conceptions of the good and of the necessary vir-tues, and no place was left for debate on institutions which were assumed to be the inevitable background to the prevailing way of life. Alternative possibilities in the provision of labour were not at the time open for discussion. We think that the society which tolerated slavery was in that respect an unjust society; most of Thomas Jefferson's contemporaries in the United States, even the more reasonable of them, did not think this. We think that they were blind to the injustice, and I shall argue that we are right to think this. They thought that persons were often unjust in their treatment of slaves, but they did not think that only an unjust society could tolerate slavery. Is it not irrational and arrogant of us to be sure that we are right and they are wrong? Ought we not rather to say that slavery was not an unjust institution in Athens or America, given the way of life and the supporting moral and metaphysical ideas of the time; rather the institution became unjust when the way of life changed together with its supporting moral ideas? A philosophical relativist speaks of justice, past and present, in this style, but the style seems to me to be inappropriate. We need to consider what the so-called blindness of reasonable persons is.

There are two ways in which we can ask about the justice or injustice of a particular practice or institution. First, we can ask whether a practice, abstracted from any set of historical conditions and considered by itself, is just or unjust. Sometimes there will be a determinate answer to this question, sometimes not, because the only possible answer in some cases is "It depends on the surrounding conditions and on the other morally significant features of particular societies." Suppose that slavery is in all conceivable conditions unjust, as I believe, and that there are good grounds for rejecting Aristotle's defences and other well-known defences of the institution; then it follows that any society which licences the practice of slavery is, to that extent and in that respect, unjust, even though the whole way of life, which includes toleration of slavery, may be in some other respects admirable. Another way of asking about justice is "Was the system of British colonial administration in Africa at the turn of the century an unjust system, taken as a whole?" or "Would it be unfair in existing conditions to increase children's allowances which could only be done at the expense of the childless?" These are complicated but not entirely abstract questions, and they could not reasonably be answered by anyone who lacked a thorough knowledge of the surrounding social conditions and of the practicable alternatives to the practices in question.

The blindness of those who did not see the injustice of slavery in the southern United States before the question was effectively raised, and before public arguments began, was an inability to abstract themselves sufficiently from their own way of life, and to ask, first, the abstract question "Is slavery in itself an injustice?" and second, "In our society as it is, is this injustice counterbalanced by some greater good?" Every person and every social group is to a greater or lesser extent blind to many of the injustices of its time, because its own culture and education, supporting a particular way of life, represents embedded and distinctive features of this way of life as unavoidable features of human life in general. So absolute monarchy, harsh conditions of labour in mines and factories, slavery, the subordination of women; so in our time the accumulation of vast fortunes in industrial countries, which can be used for political purposes and to consolidate the power and influence of wealth. No doubt our grandchildren will ask, "How can they have failed to see the injustice of allowing billionaires to multiply while the very same economy allowed abject poverty to persist uncorrected next-door to preposterous luxury?" The answer is that for many people the abstract question does not present itself as an intelligent question to ask, since the maldistribution has been represented to them as an uncontrollable natural phenomenon, like the subjection of women, and therefore the question has no relation to practicalities. The alternative possibilities, perhaps identifiable in retrospect, are not envisaged as real possibilities. The question will be effectively raised only when and if an organised social group is strongly pressing its own claims in the name of elementary justice, and when its influence and arguments can make radical redistribution of wealth a real possibility to be debated. Then the alleged injustice will be weighed against any moral costs likely to be involved in correcting it. The issue has then come alive as fit for practical reasoning.

A historian may plausibly argue that in Europe, at least since Machiavelli and Hobbes wrote, the sphere of practical reasoning in politics has been steadily and constantly extended at the expense of those imaginative pictures of human relations which are characteristic of the medieval Church, and of various pious sects and communities: pictures, for example, that associated justice and fairness in relations between social groups with a cosmic justice and harmony. The notions of degrees, and of a stratified social order, were often supported by a non-empirical and deeply imaginative picture of the cosmic order, and of God's original design. This modelling of the social order on a supernatural order was too entrenched in shared languages and vocabularies to be exposed to practical reasoning. Rather it was the assumed background to practical reasoning about social justice. For many centuries unargued notions of legitimacy, and of the inheritance of privileges and of grace, remained unalterable facts of the natural order. How else should you identify persons and understand them as persons, and how should they primarily conceive of themselves, except in terms of legitimate descent and of inherited status and role? A large shift in the non-rational, or imaginative, presuppositions of a culture or community has to occur before such images of the self are open to challenge by practical reasoning about justice. For the contemporaries of Hooker and Shakespeare the relevant notions of just subordination were built into the vocabulary rather than open to rational adversary argument.

To repeat: the contrast between "rational" and "imaginative" is intended to bring with it a contrast between a pattern of thought that is potentially common to the species and a pattern of thought that is tied to a particular language and culture, involving images and metaphors prevalent in that culture. The development of the physical sciences and of modern mathematics since 1600 spread those patterns of thought which are potentially, and in intention, frontier-crossing, and new methods of communication redoubled this effect. But it would be an error, the error of Condorcet and of Comtean positivism, to expect that rational, and therefore potentially species-wide, patterns of thought may perhaps gradually displace the language-bound and culture-bound images of the social order and of human relations. There is no more present possibility of this than that Esperanto will replace English, French, and Italian in daily use. From childhood we think, hope, and have expectations predominantly in our own language, and our emotions and desires are grown, shaped, and pruned in this linguistic home, sometimes perhaps stunted, like Japanese bonsai trees. Most important of all, our unconscious memories, and therefore our imaginations, are entangled with images of a particular place and time and with the words and images of some local past.

The concept of justice itself requires that the contrast should be preserved between rational, and potentially species-wide, patterns of thought and the culture-bound or language-bound patterns. There is no way in which entirely abstract arguments from the bare concept of justice can by themselves produce a determinate conclusion about the justice of a particular social practice, unless the imaginary court, scene of the argument, can refer to prevailing conceptions of justice which have to be taken as the starting-point of the argument. The basic concept of justice, taken by itself, is primarily procedural, prescribing that there must be a careful and unbiassed weighing of arguments on both sides. The two sides, the ayes and the nays, are supplied with the raw material for argument by the practices, the moral principles, and the precedents that prevail in a particular culture or community.

Suppose that one is asked to design a scale of wages and salaries for various occupations which will be fair and just in the differentials proposed. If the question is asked in the abstract, without reference to any particular society in which the scale is to be applied, some general principles of fairness might perhaps be suggested: for example, that some compensation is owed for the skill required and the difficulty of the work, and for its degree of unpleasantness or monotony. But such principles are too vague and general and too far removed from practical choices, until we apply them to an actual tariff of rewards in an actual society together with the moral assumptions and practices prevailing in that society, which have been taken to support the existing wage scale. For instance, what type of work has in fact been admired, and thought most desirable? Has manual work, and particularly strenuous manual work, been considered intrinsically inferior to intellectual work? Have scholars been considered particularly noble and distinguished specimens of humanity, vastly superior, for instance, to actors and singers? Which kinds of product are considered luxuries? There has to be a kind of case law of moral assumptions from which the arguments can start and to which the principles can be critically applied. After the application of the principles, which in the abstract seemed plausible, to the actual practices, many of the prevailing moral assumptions, which had supported the practices, may come to seem questionable; and equally some of the abstract principles may come to be judged questionable or wrong. For example, impressed by the principle that unpleasant work should be differentially compensated, one might conclude that underground coal-miners should be paid much more than professors, and that this is only fair. Evidently there may be moral considerations other than justice which ought to enter into the determination of wages: utility, for instance. But the possibility of deliberately adjusting wages in accordance with a principle of compensation has become arguable, a matter of practical reasoning, while hitherto it had been assumed to be in the nature of things that a professor should be paid more than a coal-miner. The other possibility did not present itself as a real possibility within the existing social structure.

Reply to Relativism

❡ I am arguing against the philosophical relativist, who insists that practices and actions are never just or unjust absolutely and without further qualification. They are just or unjust, he claims, only conditionally, given the norms of justice in a particular society, and only in relation to these norms. There is no independent standpoint, he claims, from which the conceptions of justice dominant in particular societies can be judged as more or less right or wrong, and so be judged by reference to the bare concept of justice. The reply is:

1. There is a basic concept of justice which has a constant connotation and core sense, from the earliest times until the present day; and it always refers to a regular and reasonable procedure of weighing claims and counter-claims, as in an arbitration or court of law. The procedure is designed to avoid destructive conflict. The just and rational procedure can be used in arbitrating both between competing interests and between competing moral claims.

2. The arguments supporting the contrary claims are drawn from moral assumptions and approved practices which have to some extent prevailed hitherto. The arguments proceed by a kind of appeal to accepted cases of injustice: Can you not see that having slaves is unjust, because it entails treating people as if they were domestic animals, and as not fully human? Will you not see that factory labour, left unregulated, is in effect like slave labour, when the workers have only their labour to sell? Will you not see that women, no less than men, are capable of useful work and of thought, of discovery and of creation, and that it is unjust that they should not have equal opportunities? History shows that these appeals to alleged parallels and precedents elicit counter-arguments which deny the similarities claimed. Normally the counter-argument alleges that the practice or institution under challenge exists in the nature of things, and that no alternative to it is a real possibility.

3. Conceptions of justice are constantly changing as practical reasoning enters new and unexpected domains of practice and of social life. If I am asked "Was the institution of slavery, as it existed in ancient Athens, unjust?" I reply "Yes, it was, though it did not come into conflict with the substantial conceptions of justice and of the good prevailing at the time. It was unjust be-

cause it involved treating human beings as less than fully human." Before the Stoics and Christians appeared, this argument would not have been convincing, partly because the concept of humanity admitted of degrees, and partly because slaves were not represented as complete human beings, and also because humanity was not associated with freedom of choice but rather with rationality. To the question "Is the co-existence within the same economy, and sometimes within the same neighbourhood, of great wealth and extreme poverty and malnutrition an injustice that ought to be corrected?" I think the answer is "Yes, it is, because it is only fair that vital needs should be satisfied before luxuries are provided, and we recognise the justice of this in other contexts." The primary counter-argument now would probably be that the notion of justice is out of place here, because the co-existence of great wealth and poverty is the natural consequence of any efficient economy.

4. The denial of relativism does not entail a denial that questions about justice are always matters of opinion, opinion supported by arguments from analogies with admitted cases of injustice. This is the normal pattern of practical reasoning both in law and in morality.

5. The concept of justice, like the concept of art or the concept of intelligence, has a history of being associated with different conceptions of justice, attached to different conceptions of the good. But this does not entail that the statement that a practice is, or was, unjust is always an elliptical way of saying that, given a certain conception of justice, the practice was unjust.

If in a museum I see, first, a sculpted figure from archaic Greece and, later, a Giacometti bronze figure, I may think them both magnificent works of art, even though the conceptions of art, and of visual representation, which they satisfy are radically different. I need to understand and to enter into both conceptions of visual representation in order to feel their excellence as works of art. But I can, and normally do, kick away the ladder by which I have climbed up to my aesthetic response. I do not need to say "This is a splendid work of art, given the conceptions of representation prevailing in archaic Greece or in post-Cubist, post-Surrealist Paris." If I were asked to state the features present in each of these works which made them great works of art, I should be in difficulties, as I would be in the analogous case of justice. Anything that I could say, abstracting from the particular conceptions of representation embodied in the work, would probably be rather too abstract and too general to be useful to anyone who wants guidance in understanding works of art. For the same reasons I cannot extract from the concept of substantial, as opposed to procedural, justice any informative criterion which is applicable throughout history, any more than I can extract from the concept of art an informative criterion which is applicable in every room of the museum. On the other hand neither of the two concepts is empty. There are reasons why an object can be properly included in the museum when other pleasing objects might be excluded as not worthy works of art at all. Similarly, there are reasons why the issue of injustice might be raised about a certain policy, while in other superficially similar cases this evaluation might be out of place.

The analogy between the two concepts can be used as a guide, because both concepts are normative concepts, both concepts are of their nature centres of untrivial dispute, both have a known history, and both have entered into philosophy. Every successive conception of justice, like every successive conception of the art of visual representation, has contributed something to the conceptions which have established themselves later in the history of the same societies. This is why it is possible to speak of arguments which resemble arguments from past cases in a law court. To argue that a practice or a government action is unjust is usually to point to a close analogy, or similarity, to practices already generally admitted to be unjust in the same country. But it would be a mistake, though a natural one, to conclude that there is steady progress in expanding the areas of recognised injustice. Macaulay and Lecky, and other nineteenth-century thinkers, might draw this conclusion, perhaps unconsciously influenced by the example of the physical sciences and of their attached technologies, which do indeed have an in-built tendency towards progress, unless they are interrupted by a catastrophe. But in our century of hideous atrocities, and of the flaunting of injustice, a comparison with the development of art, particularly visual art, will seem to correspond more nearly to the realities of history: a gain in sensitiveness to injustice in one set of practices is often accompanied by increasing indifference to injustice in other areas; and we cannot reasonably project a straight line of increasing respect for all forms of justice into the future. As in the arts, there may always be further relapses into barbarism, even in the more politically sophisticated and advanced countries. Certainly the mere existence of constitutional democracy in a country has not proved sufficient, even if it generally proves necessary, to preserve respect for justice in the administration of the law or to preserve social justice.

On the other hand both the concept of justice and the concept of art have been immeasurably enriched by the accumulation of past conceptions, and by our knowledge of this past and our philosophical reflections upon it. In our relation to both concepts we stand on the shoulders of our predecessors, who were either innovators, as artists and reformers, or they were consolidators, artists and theorists who developed the innovations and integrated them with the past. We are in a position to use an extended past to correct the future, at least in theoretical discussions of justice and morality, if not also in practical politics. One ought to be better able to see approaching barbarism, the march of the moral philistine, before it is too late.

Nazism and Evil

❡ The Russian Revolution and the National Socialist ascendancy in Germany are the two most important sources of evidence for moral philosophy in our time, as the French Revolution was for Hegel and Marx, and later for Tocqueville and for Mill. Although both revolutions produced, both in intention and in effect, a triumph of injustice on a gigantic scale, there are often-remarked differences between the evil effects planned and achieved. First, the Russian Revolution retained, in its published defences, some echo of the rhetoric of social justice from which its original inspiration had come. Second, the political and social system of Russia in 1917 contained more evident injustices than the political and social system in Germany in 1933, and in retrospect this affects the balance of evil. It remains true that Stalin's government was a source of injustice and destruction on a scale that has no precedent. The National Socialist revolution was from the beginning primarily aimed at injustice and world-wide domination; that was always its intention and that was its near-achievement. The intention was conceived and executed in one of the most philosophically sophisticated countries in Europe. The plan was pure evil and the realisation was a realisation of pure evil, with scarcely any counterbalancing good.

"Evil" is not a term that has been prominent in contemporary philosophical ethics: partly perhaps because the word has been associated principally with theological ethics; partly perhaps because of the unlucky obsession, at least since Moore's *Principia Ethica* in 1903, with the meanings and implications of the word "good". The notion of evil is the idea of a force, or forces, which are not merely contrary to all that is most praiseworthy and admirable and desirable in human life, but a force which is actively working against all that is praiseworthy and admirable. Evidently there are greater and lesser evils, as there are primary, greater goods and lesser goods. If one is justified in speaking of a pure evil, then one is speaking of a great evil which brings with it no good thing and which destroys without benefit, as Aristotle might speak of a purely good thing, desirable without qualification and without accompanying cost, such as health and wisdom. The National Socialist movement in Germany is an instructive case for moral philosophy, as a historical embodiment of pure evil both in aspiration and achievement. If one follows the liberal tradition of Mill, Sidgwick, G. E. Moore, and John Rawls, one is liable to think of great public evils as a falling away from the pursuit of justice or of the good, whether it be happiness, or good states of mind, or the realisation of primary goods, such as liberty: as if we had to understand those actions and policies which we consider purely evil as being the loss of those things which we consider just or good. But it is equally possible to interpret, and to understand, the things we consider primary goods as being the prevention of great evils. We may come to understand our concept of liberty best if we interpret it as the prevention both of frustration and of tyranny, which in themselves are two distinct evils. When one reflects on the Nazi movement, one may come to understand better, and to identify more distinctly, the ordinary and indispensable decencies of public life which may be overlooked in the projection of liberal ideas of social improvement. Illiberal moralists, and particularly the greatest of them, Machiavelli and Hobbes, still retain their hold on us, because they convey a vivid sense of the forces of destruction which are always at large and which have to be diverted and controlled, if any kind of decent civilised life is to continue.

Of all moral concepts it is particularly the concept of justice that cannot be fully understood without a consideration of the forces of destruction to which the virtue of justice, both in private and in public life, is meant to be an obstruction. There is a sense in which justice, both procedural and substantial, can be called a negative virtue, whether it is applied to individuals or to institutions or to policies: it is negative, in comparison with love and friendship, or courage, or intelligence. One has to ask, in a Hobbesian spirit, what it prevents rather than what it engenders. For those who studied the Nazis in the war and who thought about them afterwards, the material is at hand.

The Nazi revolution was a revolution of destruction, and, more particularly, of moral destruction: the revolution of *Nihilismus,* the title of Hermann Rauschning's book on the Nazis, which was the most clear-headed of the books written by those who knew the movement from the inside. The aim was to eliminate all notions of fairness and justice from practical politics, and, as far as possible, from person's minds; to create a bombed and flattened moral landscape, in which there are no boundaries and no limits, as in the remembered no-man's-land of the First World War. This would leave a dizzying sense in German minds that all things are possible and that nothing is forbidden and off-limits, and that there is an infinite moral space now open for natural violence and domination. There would be a liberation into a great vacancy, a moral void, as in a city that has been carpet-bombed, and the old bourgeois urbanity would be destroyed. The deliberate aim was to substitute physical conflict and violence for fair and even-handed arbitration in settling social conflicts, or in settling oppositions between races, or states, or social groups. Judicial procedures, and their established methods of argument, whether in parliament or in courts, were to be pushed out of the way, whenever they stand in the way of the party or the race. There was to be action rather than argument and talk, both now despised, and there was to be conflict without end until there is no enemy left anywhere in the world who is not subdued.

One can say without exaggeration that the aim was to invert all the values contained in the concept of justice: argument on two sides, respected procedures of gathering evidence, impartial adjudication, the avoidance of violence, distribution of rewards and penalties in accordance with rationally defensible and well-established criteria. Revenge was to be substituted for justice in relation to enemies, loyalty to party and to race was to replace impartiality, and favour and maltreatment were to depend on a person's origins rather than on his character. The weak and the handicapped and helpless minorities were to be destroyed, rather than helped, injustice again being converted into a virtue. In the style of Thrasymachus in Plato's *Republic,* but more fully worked out, justice was to be identified with the interest of the more powerful, and the exercise of power was to require no justification and to admit no restraint.

It was consistent to put the elimination of Jews from the state at the centre of the programme. Having been always excluded from the land-owning and military classes, many Jews in Europe had turned towards scholarly, intellectual, argumentative interests and had elaborated systems of law of great complexity. Their morality was a morality of literacy and of legality, which required them to submit their lives to the law, fully articulated over the centuries and interpreted by the learned, whose learning earned them the respect of the community. Strict observance of the law had been combined with an inherited delight in ingenuity of legal and quasi-legal argument, and in the disputable interpretations of texts. If martial arts are excluded, habits of aggressive argument, and of intellectual ingenuity, naturally take their place. From commercial practice, highly developed because of their exclusion from land-owning, the Jews had over the centuries developed a delight in dealing and in negotiation, a delight which is also a feature of other commercial cultures, as among Greeks in the Roman Empire. Jews had in the Old Testament represented their relation with God as a continuing negotiation within the law, and this was the tradition which Kafka both prolonged and parodied in his stories. Justice, both in God's judgment and in the law to be observed among humans, was the central moral concept for the Jews, the very reverse of all that the Nazis wanted. The National Socialist programme was to destroy in Germany both the morality of literacy and of legality and the morality of fair negotiation. They wanted no more arguments, no more justice: just the excitement of conflict and of victory through violence.

Below any level of explicit articulation, hatred of the idea of the Jews was tied to hatred of the power of intellect, as opposed to military power, hatred of law courts, of negotiation, of cleverness in argument, of learning and of the domination of learning: and in this way anti-Semitism is tied to hatred of justice itself, which must set a limit to the exercise of power and to domination.

Throughout the Christian era and in this century there have been other episodes of genocide, wars of religion leading to famine and massacre, and many outbursts of tribal hatred. For most parts of the world and in most centuries, a population living under a rule of law which was backed by some plausible conceptions of justice has been unusually fortunate. But at least from the age of Grotius until the advent of Fascism, lip-service had been paid in Europe to inherited principles of justice, some of which had their origin with Aristotle and some of which had been preserved by the churches up to and after the Reformation. The significance of National Socialism, in the context of moral philosophy, is, first, that it was an explicit and direct exaltation of injustice and of violence at the expense of justice, with a sinister minimum of hypocrisy and lip-service; second, that the rise to power of the Nazis came after a period in which liberal and secular conceptions of justice, traceable to the French Revolution, had spread through much of Europe, carried on a wave of middle-class prosperity with a corresponding decline of aristocratic moralities. The Nazi fury to destroy had a definite target: the target encompassed reasonableness and legality and the procedures of public discussion, justice for minorities, the protection of the weak, and the protection of human diversity.

Historians will show how this happened and perhaps even try to explain why it happened. The philosophical interest is also a historical interest: for instance, in the replacement of the idea of justice by the idea of liberty as the dominant concept in political morality during the nineteenth century, not only among Hegelians and Marxists, but also among liberals and radicals. The identification, or at least association, of improvement and progress with the extension of liberty persisted from Rousseau and the Jacobins through J. S. Mill up to the present day, and it is conspicuous again in Rawls's *A Theory of Justice*. Liberty, like happiness and the pursuit of happiness, is a positive ideal, while justice is a negative ideal. To recommend practices and institutions in proportion as they remove barriers to the freedom of individuals is to aim at a positive good. The aim is one of enlightened improvement in harmony with those human desires which can be assumed to be almost universal. We think of justice as a restraint upon those desires: the desire for a greater share of rewards, the desire for dominance. It is the denial of pleonexia, as Plato wrote, of getting more than is due, of unmeasured ambition, of over-reaching, and of self-assertion without limit. When justice needs to be enforced and is enforced, the scene is not one of harmony; some ambitions are frustrated. A barrier is erected, an impossibility declared.

Basic Procedural Justice

❡ There is a basic level of morality, a bare minimum, which is entirely negative, and without this bare minimum as a foundation no morality directed towards the greater goods can be applicable and can survive in practice. A rock-bottom and preliminary morality of justice and fair dealing is needed to keep a balance between competing moralities and to support respected procedures of arbitration between them. Otherwise any society becomes an unstable clash of fanaticisms. Procedural justice is for this reason a necessary support of any morality in which more positive virtues are valued. Justice is even more indispensable to morality than courage, because there could be a scholarly and withdrawn way of life, with its supporting virtues, which would only in very exceptional circumstances require acts of courage: not so for justice, always required.

Plato in the *Republic* represented justice as the social bond made necessary by the division of labour and the specialisation of functions. He represented the three different ways of life of the three classes in the city as each contributing to a single supreme good which all would fully or partially share. Neither Plato nor Aristotle, nor Kant, nor any utilitarian, would tolerate a denial that there is one supreme good for human beings. In the next two chapters I shall defend this denial, which I hold to be essential in understanding why the negative virtue of procedural justice is the necessary foundation of any particular set of virtues supporting any particular way of life, whatever that way of life may be. In many societies, and particularly in modern states, the difference between ways of life within a single society cannot plausibly be represented as contributing to a common good. The different ways of life are buttressed by contrary and irreconcilable beliefs, usually religious, but sometimes also purely moral. In any large and economically developed society there will be a battle, not only of conflicting interests, but also of contrary moral ideals, passionately defended. The contrary conceptions of the essential virtues and of the best way of life will also include divergent conceptions of justice itself. This must happen, because each conception of the best way of life entails some duties and forbearances, supporting that particular way of life, and some of these duties will fall under the heading of justice.

For example, what counts as the fair and just treatment of children will depend upon the conception of their ultimate interests, and of the interests of the family, and these conceptions must be part of a particular idea of the best way of life. Similarly what counts as the just and fair treatment of foreigners will vary with different conceptions of citizenship and of the importance of the state in the best way of life: this will be very different for a cosmopolitan liberal, who recognises a duty not to discriminate between citizens and foreigners more than is necessary for administrative reasons, and for the person who attaches very great value to the solidarity and the historical continuity and the individual character of the community in which he or she lives. To such a person it seems only fair that a foreigner should recognise the right of a community to protect its national and cultural identity against the intrusion of foreigners into its intimate affairs.

For this reason a bare minimum concept of justice, underlying all the distinct, specific, and substantial conceptions, is indispensable, if there is to be a peaceful and coherent society. Evidently the difficulty is to specify what this minimum concept of justice ought to be, given that it must be independent of specific, and therefore divisive, conceptions of the good.

Hobbes's problem of reconciling rationally competing appetites for safety, liberty, and power was less difficult than the problem of finding a fair and just procedure in arbitrating between competing conceptions of fairness and justice, each dependent on a specific conception of the good. The solution must resemble

Hobbes's in finding a common ground in a common human situation which calls for a shared use of practical reasoning, for a minimum rationality. War, conflict, and hostility of all kinds have their limits, and sometimes they will end, not in conquest and domination, but in negotiation and compromise. Negotiation, in common with all occasions of argument, involves recognised rules and customs as a condition of its existence. The notion of fairness enters in, conspicuously in the swapping of concessions, when a fair exchange is required in the interests of compromise, and when both sides need to live together in some kind of peace. The notion of fairness associated with negotiations is so far a minimum procedural fairness, which is an essential part of the concept of justice. Two specific conceptions of justice are to be presented and applied to a particular case, with full deployment of supporting arguments. The conditions of adversary argument will not grossly favour one side, if the negotiation is to be a fair one. Obviously custom and historical circumstances dictate a host of specific conditions of fairness governing any particular negotiation.

When natural enemies sit down to negotiate, whether they are individuals or governments, we find them calling on a quasi-legal fairness as a respected requirement in their arguments as, for example, in negotiations between the United States and the Soviet Union. In international negotiation, and in negotiation between hostile political groups more generally, procedural fairness, particularly fairness in balancing concession against concession, is the only respected restraint upon the unmoralised manoeuvres of realpolitik. Negotiation when there are moral conflicts is no less an evident necessity in human affairs than friendship is, and there can be no effective negotiation without cross-frontier and therefore rational standards of fairness in argument. For each type of negotiation, and in each context of negotiation, there is a heritage of customs and rules which determine the fair and appropriate procedure for that type, and which determine what counts as an equal concession and as a fair compromise. Universal and abstract principles of justice will under-determine what counts as equal and as fair dealing in the widely various contexts of negotiation. But the parties who enter any negotiation are not inventing the practices for the first time and their expectations of just procedures are based on precedents that fit the present context. The tangled web of recognised procedures of negotiation and exchange constitutes the social bond that holds a people together, outside family circles; and even the nursery is a scene of negotiation and exchange, of disputed fairness in the swapping of goods, of precedent-setting in adjudication, and of compromise.

When Hitler and the Nazi leaders deliberately substituted force, and the threat of force, for negotiation in dealing with other groups and parties in Germany, they knew that they were creating a pliant and demoralised mass, ready and fit for domination. Both in the middle class and in the working class customary procedures of negotiation and adjudication between opposing interests were the core of public morality. When the use of force proved successful, and all the conventions of negotiation had been swept away, morality itself had been destroyed in public affairs. Morality survived in families, among friends, in professions, and perhaps in commerce. In Paris under the Jacobins, a new conception of justice was substituted for the old, at least in intention and to some extent in reality; but in Nazi Germany there was to be no morality in government. An abyss was opened. The only reality in public affairs was to be pure domination and pure subjection, with no outrage forbidden and no limit set.

The abolition of justice in public life, and therefore the abolition of morality itself in public life, very nearly succeeded in Europe, and was blocked only by the Battle of Stalingrad and later by the British and American armies in France. This real possibility of absolute evil now remains a challenge to moral philosophy which cannot be conjured away. Not only is any particular morality fragile and always dependent for its survival in practice on contingent historical circumstances; but morality itself, the whole range of practices and institutions classifiable as moralities, is fragile.

Anyone who interrogated and talked to leading Nazis, and who studied the methods of Hitler's SS in occupied territories, and even those who read *Mein Kampf,* are unlikely to be convinced by those philosophical relativists who represent Hitler and Nazi leaders as introducing a new morality, replacing liberal and Christian moralities of all kinds. A will to destruction so simple, so single-minded, and so free from conflict cannot reasonably be accounted a sort of morality. Even the most drastic and reductive utilitarian is not so simple-minded as to eliminate the moral conflicts that arise from the balancing of short-term against long-term utilities, one group against another, quantities against intensities. Utilitarians generally expect to reproduce in their revised moral terms many of the difficult conflicts of claims which are typical of conventional morality. Hitler, and his thousands of devoted followers, were furiously impatient with all moral complexities and anxieties as such, and were determined to destroy in Germany, once and for all, the tradition of moral and disputable limits in the pursuit of power.

Historians and social anthropologists can certainly cite harsh moral and religious doctrines that naturally led to great destruction of life and to widespread repression and misery. For example, one can cite some religious or metaphysical enthusiasm which inspired a crusade and the destruction of the infidel and the unconverted. This would be a case of gross injustice and moral outrage perpetrated in the name of some higher justice, supernaturally endorsed: a case of an evil morality. The originality of Hitler, in dismissing all moral restraints, was the consequence of his arriving so late in European history, well after the theorists of realpolitik and after the many misinterpretations of Nietzsche. The only possible example of an evil morality in Hitler's programme is its racism, which had some features of a moral crusade. It seems possible that sometimes—conspicuously in Russia—his plans for world domination were knowingly modified, and jeopardised, by racist principles. In so far as this is true, and in so far as racist principles were for him more than a means of uniting his followers against a common target, I would acknowledge that Nazism had an element of evil morality alongside the single-minded pursuit of domination.

The known successes of the Nazi movement in Germany and elsewhere ought to have destroyed forever a previous innocence in moral philosophy: an innocence which is evident in Mill and Sidgwick and G. E. Moore, but which extends backwards in time to the first utilitarians, and even to Hume and Adam Smith and to other British moralists of their century. They wrote as if it was sufficient to establish some truths about the great goods for mankind, and then to deduce from these truths the necessary human virtues and vices and the necessary social policies. It is not sufficient, because there is a distinct and prior necessity, which does not follow directly from any account of the great goods, and which remains a necessity, whichever of these great goods is affirmed and in whatever order of priority. The universal necessity of basic procedural justice, as a reasonable and arguable restraint upon the natural drive to domination, has to be recognised as contrasting with the variety of great goods acknowledged in different moralities. The contrast is so great that it justifies talking of two aspects of morality: the universal and the particular. Practicing Christians of all kinds, Moslems of all kinds, Orthodox Jews of all kinds, Marxists of all kinds, atheistical liberals of all kinds, atheistical conservatives of all kinds, recognise that their conceptions of the good are in some respects incompatible and mutually hostile, and that this must be so, if their conceptions have any specific content. That they should convert unbelievers (or non-sceptics) to their way of thinking may, or may not, be part of any one of these moral persuasions: rationality does not require a drive to conversion, nor does it require its opposite. But if it is true that an unrestrained natural drive to domination is the greatest source of evil, and if evil here is neutrally interpreted as involving destruction of life, oppression, and misery, then it is rational for each and all of the moral sectaries to look for a non-divisive and generally acceptable conception of justice, however thin a conception this may be, amounting at its minimum only to fair procedures of negotiation.

3

Hume's Ghost

⟨ This is the point at which the ample and amiable ghost of Hume, never to be avoided in moral philosophy, makes his appearance, sceptically smiling. He makes three clear observations, two about moral values in general, observations closely related to each other, and one about the virtue of justice in particular. First, he argues that if we just gaze at the world, abstracting from our own feelings, and then ask ourselves what is good and what is just, no credible and respectworthy answer will be forthcoming. Good and evil, and other values, are not perceived features in nature or in the external world, as shapes and colours are. As we naturally project our feelings of pleasure and displeasure onto things, characterising them as pleasant and unpleasant, so we project our sentiments of approval and disapproval onto things, characterising them as good or bad.

Second, he claims that it is not "contrary to reason" for me to prefer the destruction of the whole world to the smallest injury to my finger. It is a matter of natural feeling and sentiment. Third, he asserts that people do not have any direct and immediate feeling for justice, which is in this sense an artificial virtue, unlike benevolence. An interest in justice needs to be induced by calculation of consequences and by sympathy with suffering.

To take these points in the reverse order: it seems to me empirically false that there is no observable, natural, and immediate feeling about unfairness and fairness—for example, in young children. This feeling is particularly evident in distributive justice, which imposes penalties and distributes rewards. The feeling, which is usually at least as strong as feelings of sympathy, does not seem to have been induced by imitation or by persuasion or by propaganda. Hume, like Hobbes, was under the spell of a pseudo-Newtonian picture of the self as set in motion only by simple and self-serving drives. His assertion is in any case too general and too vague to be easily testable. I shall give other reasons for claiming that justice is a natural virtue, no less than benevolence and no less than the disposition to sympathise with the suffering of others.

The first two claims, taken together, are a denial that moral judgments can be true, and rationally defensible, statements about their apparent subjects: persons, actions, feelings, policies, laws, institutions. When they are compared with ordinary empirical statements about the external world—external, that is, to human feelings and attitudes—moral judgments can be seen to convey no truths about the external world itself; they convey only truths about human feelings about the external world. That was Hume's claim. For reasons given in Chapter 1, this seems to me a false account of value judgments in general and of moral judgments in particular; more specifically, it implies a false account of predications of good. As regards the second claim, evidently Hume was entitled, as a philosopher pursuing a systematic theory of knowledge, to confine the phrase "contrary to reason" to rigorous contexts of argument, contexts that occur only in logic and mathematics and in closely related disciplines. But if he wished to draw some substantial consequences from his aphorism, he was relying on an error in the philosophy of language, the error of false isolation. I shall call this error of false isolation "Hume's trick", because he uses it with famous effect in several contexts.

False Isolation

❡ A parallel drawn from ordinary empirical statements will illustrate the error. Suppose I say that, once the brake is released, this automobile must of necessity run into the wall downhill from it, and you reply, "Perhaps not; there might be an earthquake", and I ascertain that you do not believe that there has ever been an earthquake here, or that there is ever in the least likely to be. Then you have not so far given me any grounds for repudiating, or for doubting, my statement, which is of a type that presupposes that familiar constancies in the world will remain constant. In evaluating such standard conditional judgments, above a minimum level of complexity, certain constancies, implied by the context of the discourse, are presupposed as the background before the acceptability of the statement can be assessed. The classic example of suspending such presuppositions for special philosophical purposes is Cartesian doubt, or rather one form of Cartesian doubt. When I say "I know for sure that this is my hand out-stretched in front of me," you might reply, "No, you do not know for sure: you might be dreaming about an outstretched hand." Admitting that there is not the smallest, ten-thousand-to-one chance that I am dreaming at the moment in question, you still insist that there is always the theoretical possibility of it, and that therefore one can never know for sure anything of this kind; you have withdrawn the phrase "know for sure" from its normal use, by cancelling the normal presupposition of the expected constancies in the world. Similarly for Hume's statement that it is not contrary to reason to prefer the destruction of the whole world: if you stare at this strange normative sentence, taken in isolation from the various contexts of thought in which you would expect to meet it, you will not know what special background conditions you are supposed to assume in place of the normal ones; and under those conditions you will be unable to evaluate the statement as acceptable or unacceptable, as true or false. Just as events can be judged to be either necessary or possible, only given the presupposition, appropriate to the context, of certain constancies in nature as a background, so actions and practices can be judged to be reasonable, or contrary to reason, only given the standard presuppositions about certain rough constancies in human nature. In both cases a general and vague *ceteris paribus* clause is always presupposed and normally not explicitly stated.

There is no good reason to impute to moral judgments some indeterminacy which is peculiar to them. The same presumption of background knowledge of unquestioned constancies is made with causal judgments and singular counterfactual conditional judgments of many kinds, as with moral judgments of many different kinds. When the English word "judgment" is in place as applied to a statement, there will usually be a strong background presupposition which has to be understood before the statement can be assessed as true or false, acceptable or unacceptable. These judgments about possibilities can be contrasted with a type of statement which can be assessed as true or false with only the minimum of presupposed background. An example would be the record in a ship's log-book: statements such as "At 12.00 hours some fog to starboard"; "At 12.05 hours tanker sighted at anchor to port." Such singular categorical statements can be called semantically simple, as opposed to the semantically complex types of statement just listed. The list of complex types should include all singular counterfactual judgments, and modal judgments involving "must" and "ought", whether judgments of nomic necessity or moral necessity or epistemic necessity.

Hume's trick was to induce his readers to stare at a semantically complex judgment taken in isolation from its normal context in a particular type of discourse and therefore disconnected from the presupposed background to its evaluation. He performed the trick with causal judgments and then again with evaluative judgments, and with judgments involving an "ought". Semantically simple statements, such as log-book records, are comparatively unproblematical, while causal, modal, and evaluative statements, which are properly called judgments, are problematical. They are problematical in the sense that you cannot tell under what conditions the statement is to be evaluated as true or false, acceptable or unacceptable, just by looking at the wording of the sentence, or at the apparent sense of the statement, taken in isolation.

Hume performed his trick of disconnection in psychological terms as well as in logico-linguistic terms. I can directly and immediately perceive the colour of a thing, but I cannot directly and immediately perceive myself changing the colour of the thing with my paintbrush; this would involve perceiving a necessary connection. "There is a patch of blue" can be evaluated on the ocular evidence alone; "I am changing the colour with my paintbrush" requires some presupposed constancies about the regular behaviour of paints, brushes, and colours to be added before the ocular evidence is sufficient to justify the judgment. That is the Humean claim, contrasting causal judgments with the record of sensory impressions; knowledge of the former kind has to be inferential, even if the inference is pre-conscious, while the description of a sensory impression, such as a colour, is immediate, non-inferential, and direct. This contrast is a false one. Both kinds of statement are sometimes known to be true directly and immediately, and both are known sometimes only as the outcome of an inference. They are equally corrigible in the light of further evidence.

For the present argument the important point is Hume's false isolation of typical statements, which turns the relation between statements and beliefs on the one side, and reality on the other, upside down. Any natural phenomenon that we become aware of, whether in the external world or in our own mind, occurs in a larger setting and in a larger extra-linguistic context, both spatial and temporal, from which it needs to be abstracted and then isolated for attention and for subsequent reference and description. Aided by general categories of description and by our own vocabulary, we pick out from the continuum of experience, and render salient, features and objects which are of current interest to us. We can never completely protect our statements about salient features and about interesting individuals against the always present possibility of a mistaken reference and of a mistaken description. There is always the possibility of the environment containing some exceptional non-salient feature which makes the observed situation a non-standard and deviant one. We have to rely for the purposes of communication on a general presupposition that the relevant and sufficient evidence that supports the statement does not on this occasion leave out of account abnormal features of the situation, which undermine the worth of the evidence. For complex empirical statements to be determinately evaluated as acceptable or unacceptable on the basis of evidence, there needs to be a fence of presupposition built around them to exclude the infinite possibilities of freakish mishaps that a philosophical sceptic could mention.

Consider as a parallel statements of a person's intentions for the future, when she says what she will do tomorrow; there is a fence of presupposition that protects her statement from all the abnormal accidents that could admittedly lead her to change her mind. The statement depends on its support from the normal contingencies envisaged from inside the fence of presupposition, which excludes freakish possibilities. Statements of intention could not be made, and could not be evaluated as acceptable or unacceptable, true or false, without presupposing a limited background of relevant possibilities. A statement of intention, like a singular causal statement, abstracts from the infinite variety of conditions which might be mentioned as in principle but not in practice relevant to its acceptability or truth. She does not need to add the general clause "God willing" on every occasion: if at all, only on occasions of exceptional risk.

There is nothing mysterious about the notion of presupposition and about the effects of cancelling normal presuppositions and of thereby making the evaluation of different kinds of statement impossible. In making statements about the world, and therefore making the necessary abstraction from the totality of things, I always presuppose that both the natural world and the social world are proceeding normally, and that my statement is to be evaluated by reference to a finite and conveniently circum-scribed body of salient evidence. This salient evidence is always defective unless the conventionally presupposed constancies are added, which serve to exclude the infinite possibilities of error in any particular case. The complexity of the presuppositions is a matter of degree, extending from the minimum with the log-book to the maximum with some modal judgments. For disput-able modal statements, one presupposes that the possibilities and necessities are to be tested under well-understood normal condi-tions, and not, for example, during an earthquake or a hurricane, unless there is an earthquake zone in the case. If the court of inquiry concludes that the cause of the accident was so-and-so, its conclusion is not to be challenged by imagining some im-probable possibility which the court left out of account. Rational method in the discovery of singular causes demands that very general and unspecified *ceteris paribus* clauses are presupposed.

Consider moral judgments such as "It is not contrary to reason to prefer the destruction of the whole world to the smallest in-jury to my finger." In normal contexts, and outside the discourse of sceptical philosophy, moral judgments presuppose some rough common knowledge of constancy in normal human feel-ings. Such unspecific knowledge of the constancies in human af-fairs is the framework into which moral judgments are fitted and within which normal disputes and conflicts are expressed. If someone steps outside the presumed framework and asks "Why should it matter if mankind is painfully destroyed as the effect of a final explosion, which I admit my foreign policy makes likely?" one would for a moment be at a loss in carrying on the discussion. One would need to find out whether any constancies of human feeling, and of human interests, of any kind were being presupposed, and whether they were so far removed from the normal presuppositions as to remove the judgment from the sphere of morality altogether. One would be at a loss in the same way if a statesman admitted that his policy, in order to be effec-tive, required the occurrence of a miracle, and if he admitted that he was presuming, as a background to his empirical judgment, that there would be a divine intervention in the anticipated events. He would have spoken misleadingly, if he had not made his presumption explicit, because this is very far from being the generally presupposed background when alternative policies are discussed.

A Humean sceptic may ask why judgments of the types listed—moral, causal, counterfactual—always carry with them strong presuppositions of constancy as well as supporting evidence and why the supporting evidence is otherwise never sufficient. The answer is: for the same reason that definite descriptions used in a natural language do not secure determinacy of reference, as they can do in the formal languages of mathematics. There is always the theoretical possibility in natural languages of a definite description, without any corrigible error of the speaker, failing to identify, or identifying by mischance the wrong item. This feature of the relation of language to reality I called in *Thought and Action* "the inexhaustibility of description". Because any modal, causal, counterfactual, dispositional, or evaluative, judgment picks out salient relationships between salient features from the inexhaustible network of actual features in reality, a *ceteris paribus* clause is always needed. Take away the fence, as the Humean sceptic suggests, and no judgment of any complexity can achieve any determinacy as either true or false in the light of the evidence, because it is exposed to the infinite possibilities that can be quoted against it.

Value Judgments

❡ Consider four evaluative judgments claiming truth and objectivity: "Tolstoy was a great novelist." "Hitler's policies were absolutely evil." "An accused person must have a fair trial as a matter of right." "A powerful imagination is as important a virtue as a powerful intellect." These judgments are semantically complex, in the sense that they presuppose certain constancies in human feeling, and human interests, and human institutions, and the reasons that would be given in support of these judgments are effective as reasons only if taken in conjunction with the various presuppositions of constancy. Hume claimed that value judgments are as such no more than expressions of human feelings, just as he claimed that causal judgments ("My fingers are making the shapes") are no more than assertions about felt expectations.

Both claims depend upon a confusion between the conditions of knowing something and what is known, between presupposition and content. No one of my four value judgments expresses or entails any assertion about human feelings. It would not be strictly inconsistent to believe that Tolstoy was a great novelist and to disbelieve that the majority of his readers admired or enjoyed his novels, and it would not be strictly inconsistent to believe that Hitler was evil and to disbelieve that most people had adverse feelings about him. Human feelings enter into the assessment of the judgments in both cases only as the presupposed background that explains why the reasons to be given in support of the judgments are good reasons. The reasons that support the judgment that Tolstoy was a great novelist are to be found in features of his novels, considered as novels, and the judgment is not an assertion about human feelings, nor does it entail such an assertion; but it does entail the modal judgment "If you are interested in reading novels, you ought to read Tolstoy" (unless there is some overriding reason against reading him). The features of the novels that make it true that Tolstoy was a great novelist constitute good evidence, or good reasons, only given some very general presupposed constancies in human interests. Novel-reading plays a fairly definite part in our way of life, and this function explains why certain features are good reasons for praising a novel, as I argued in Chapter 1.

These four judgments are, I believe, true and they are in no clear sense "subjective". Like a historian's judgments about the causes of a revolution or about unrealised possibilities in the past, they are matters of opinion, of rationally confident opinion, and they are supported by reasons, more or less compelling, which obviously never amount to proofs. A historian's causal judgments presuppose some very general constancies observable in human history and in nature. Each of the four evaluative judgments presuppose also some very general constancies in human interests and institutions. If we descend from these generalities towards more specific human feelings, moral divergences naturally begin. The three moral judgments in the above list presuppose the very general constancies which mark out the range of moral discourse. Within this range, set by the common conditions of human life, there are the many moral divergences associated with different ways of life. The three judgments are all for this reason disputable; for instance, not every defensible conception of the good has a place for the concept of absolute evil, and not every defensible morality gives priority to procedural justice. I am thinking here particularly of utilitarian morality, and of other forms of consequentialist morality, which would at least qualify and amend all three judgments.

Moral relativism has always rested on an under-estimate of universal human needs, and therefore of the negative aspects of morality—as opposed to diversity in ideals and interests, diversity in conceptions of the good, which are the positive aspects of morality. There is nothing mysterious or "subjective" or culture-bound in the great evils of human experience, re-affirmed in every age and in every written history and in every tragedy and fiction: murder and the destruction of life, imprisonment, enslavement, starvation, poverty, physical pain and torture, homelessness, friendlessness. That these great evils are to be averted is the constant presupposition of moral arguments at all times and in all places, and particularly when the costs involved in pursuing different conceptions of the good are being counted. That destruction of human life, suffering, and imprisonment are, taken by themselves, great evils, and that they are evil without qualification, if nothing can be said about consequences which might palliate the evil; that it is better that persons should be free rather than starving in prisons or concentration camps—these are some of the constancies of human experience and feeling presupposed as the background to moral judgments and arguments. They correspond, as constant evils presupposed, to such constant regularities as the effects of gravity, or the alternation of night and day, presupposed in everyday natural explanation. All ways of life require protection against the great evils, even though different conceptions of the good may rank their prevention in very different orders of priority.

To summarize the reply to Hume: I am arguing that moral judgments, and specifically judgments about justice and fairness, are no less determinate and no less "objective" than empirical judgments involving "ought" and "must" and related modal notions: no less determinate, in that they are equally susceptible of being true or false, or of being acceptable or unacceptable, and that they are equally founded on evidence and reasons; no less "objective", in that the apparent subject of a moral judgment (a person, a practice, an action, a state of mind) is also the real subject. I base these conclusions on the account of predications of the good in Chapter 1, and the implications of such predications in "ought" statements and "must" statements; on the distinct recognition of the great evils, to be explained later; and on an account of the role of presuppositions in the evaluation of all complex judgments expressed in a natural language, outside the notations and contexts of mathematics and of logic. If you isolate a statement by removing it from any presupposed type of discourse, and if you suspend all presuppositions of the background knowledge appropriate to this type, then it becomes impossible to evaluate the statement. A sceptic will then suggest that the evidence, however plentiful, is grossly inadequate to support the conclusion; and indeed, without the context and the presuppositions, the evidence always is incomplete.

Why is there this need of a presupposed background of known constancies? Because of the infinite complexity of features which could be quoted, however unreasonably, as possibly relevant to the truth of the judgment, which is always an abstraction from all these complicating possibilities. Even the log-book statement of minimum semantic complexity "Fog to starboard at 5.00 P.M.", made by the observer with perfect perceptual evidence, has its presuppositions of the constancies in nature. Fog has to have a certain composition and origin to be real fog. The contrasting kind of log-book statement, which could be determinate in isolation and without any presupposition, would occur in the narrative of a chess game, already expressed in an abstract notation: "Castle to queen's pawn in move 15." The notation by itself excludes all those indefinitely many features of the events on the board which are not definable features of a chess game. The rules and conventions of the game make the necessary abstraction from the infinite complexities of the natural order.

When one moves upwards in semantical complexity from simple categorical statements to judgments about possibilities, and to judgments involving "ought" and "must", the role of presupposed constancies in securing determinacy necessarily increases. This is a familiar truth about singular counterfactuals ("Even if he is caught in heavy traffic, which is most unlikely, he ought to be here by four o'clock"), or singular causal statements ("With the ice on the wings the accident was inevitable"), or prudential statements ("You ought to be more polite, if you want to succeed"), or conditional predictions ("If you plant the seed now, it ought to flower in good time"), or moral statements ("You ought to curtail their liberties rather than risk a massacre"). We all speak to each other about such possibilities and necessities with very general *ceteris paribus* clauses in mind, and on some occasions of disagreement some of the more specific presupposed constancies are made explicit in the ensuing argument.

For all these four judgments about possible worlds, involving "ought" and "must", there is a scale of testability and determinacy. For example, causal and counterfactual judgments become comparatively indeterminate when tested uniformities are lacking ("If there had been no world depression, there would have been no Second World War"). At the other end of the scale, when the singular counterfactual specifies a confirmed universal statement ("If the bomb explodes here, we will both be dead"), the judgment is comparatively determinate, and "true" is the natural epithet to use about this statement. One might also say "That is a fact: we would both be dead", although one is talking about a possibility, not an actuality. For moral judgments maximum in-determinacy is found in the often-quoted cases in which two great evils, or two conflicting duties, are encountered and a choice has to be made, and no overriding principle can be ex-tracted from any acceptable conception of the good ("Ought I, a Jew, to play a part in the disgusting administration of the Holo-caust, if I can save many Jewish lives in the process?") At the top of the scale there might be the singular moral judgment ("He is innocent in the matter, and he ought not to be made to suffer"), which is a singular specification of a widely accepted moral prin-ciple ("You ought not to cause an innocent person to suffer un-necessarily").

This and other parallels between empirical judgments and moral judgments involving "ought" and "must" should not be found surprising. In each of the two ranges of judgment we are talking about possible worlds, which have to be constructed in thought by changing salient characteristics of the actual world, and by leaving the remaining, infinitely many, features of the actual world in place. Obviously no features of the actual world are salient except in relation to some human purpose or inquiry. We pick out the features that are to be salient and that are to count as reasons for our predictions and controlled expectations; and we similarly pick out reasons for our considered intentions and practical recommendations.

Possibilities and Presuppositions

❡ There are two distinct public situations which human beings typically encounter, and in which they learn to speak their native languages: first, the deliberative council, scene of practical rea-soning, of the balancing of reasons ("What ought we to do?" or "What must we do?"); second, the prediction of, not the choice among, possibilities (for instance, trying to predict the harvest: "If it does not rain, must the crops perish?"). Human beings never have been able, and never will be able, to live without discussing these two related types of possibility and also without silently and continuously thinking about both of them. The modal forms, involving "ought" and "must", "may" and "might", "can" and "could", must be understood as arising from these two types of predicament, sometimes distinguished as demanding either practical or theoretical reasoning. The very same sentence may convey, on different occasions of its use, first one, then the other, type of question, and the modal sentences are often ambiguous. They are only disambiguated by the contexts of discourse or conversation. The types of discourse are identified by the distinct needs to which they are a response: the need to know what will happen in the natural course of events, and the need to decide what should be done.

It was a philosophical mistake to represent belief in some proposition, called the uniformity of nature, as a necessary presupposition of using experimental methods of prediction. There is no requirement of a definite belief about the natural order. There is only the necessity of a procedure, the procedure of trial and error with next year's crops, and of consulting the record of past trials before playing poker with the god who orders the monsoon. It was the inductivist's error to affirm the uniformity of nature. Similarly, in comparing possible policies and their effects, one does not need either to assert or to imply the truth of some definite proposition of similar generality about the end of all human endeavour or the nature of happiness or about any other so-called ultimate good thing. The only universal necessities arise from the nature of the universal practice itself, the procedures of publicly and privately deliberating about possibilities. In the council chamber, there is the reasonable requirement of fairness in attending to the arguments from all sides of the council chamber, of minimum procedural justice, and a corresponding judiciousness in any internal debate, where this habit of fairness amounts to practical wisdom. This type of fairness is a precise analogue of the requirement in a theoretical inquiry that all the accessible evidence should be assembled and assessed.

From a philosophical standpoint it is necessary to insist that "ought" and "must" are univocal in their employments, including their employment in empirical judgments and in moral judgments. "Ought" and "must", typically and generally, serve to mark the contrast between speaking of actuality and speaking of possibility, and moral discourse, typically and generally, is discourse about possibilities, about worlds and persons that would be better and worse than the actual worlds and persons that we see around us. The modal words—"ought", "must", "may", "might", "can", and "could"—are univocal in the same sense that "true" and "false" are univocal in their application to statements or judgments about possibilities as well as to statements about actualities. It is unequivocally true both that he must be starving by now, and that you ought to feed him.

Fact and Value

❡ In addition to claiming that all moral judgments are really expressions of the speaker's feelings, Hume argued that there is an unbridgeable gap and disconnection between statements of fact and evaluative statements, and between statements of what is in fact the case and statements of what ought to be the case. In Chapter 1 I have argued that both claims are false, and that there cannot be such a gap and total disconnection. There is a systematic connection between the identification of a thing, and of an activity, as being of certain kind, and the identification of the thing and the activity as being good or acceptable examples of the kind. If a person does not waltz reasonably well, and if she does not execute more or less the steps that she ought to execute in a waltz, she cannot be waltzing. These entailments hold for an immense variety of different types of thing and of different types of activity, and not only for comparatively formal and rule-governed activities such as waltzing. The relation between classification and evaluation is a very general one in the common-sense, pre-theoretical, vocabulary, particularly with activities described by verbs of achievement rather than verbs of process. A person has to be skating reasonably well in order actually to be skating, rather than trying to skate. When we observe him on the ice, we see immediately what the situation is in respect of his skating. Values of this kind are directly perceived just as human struggles and attempts are perceived. We see and hear good copies, copies which are all that they ought to be, just as clearly as we see copies which are so bad that they scarcely count as copies at all.

That there is no unbridgeable gap between so-called descriptive expressions and so-called evaluative expressions is important in moral philosophy for a number of reasons. First, and contrary to Hume, some inferences are permitted within our ordinary vocabulary that start from a judgment recording an observed phenomenon and conclude with a judgment about what ought to be the case. If I hear someone singing "Caro nome" and she is halfway through the aria, I can infer what notes she ought to have sung before and what notes she ought to sing next. If both these inferences fail and neither "ought" statement is true, either it was not "Caro nome" that I heard, or it was a very bad version of "Caro nome". If there is no logical bar to valid inferences which pass from observed phenomena to "ought" statements, and to evaluations, then there is no need to look for a satisfactory criterion or method of distinguishing between so-called descriptive, or purely descriptive, predicates and evaluative predicates. It has notoriously been difficult to find a satisfactory criterion, which does not admit a great number of border-line and mongrel cases drawn from the common vocabulary.

In discussing the characters of persons, their ways of life, their virtues, and other features of their conduct, we contrive to communicate clearly and vividly our impressions of people and of their lives by applying predicates which enter easily into a number of quite different contexts: moral contexts, contexts of aesthetic evaluation, and contexts in which they are meant to be aids to recognition, and in which they are not to be taken primarily as evaluations. These are impressionistic predicates; they are not governed in their application by criteria or tests, and, in some cases, not even by evidence. In Kantian terms, they are drawn from the third and intermediate type of discourse, which is neither the scientific discourse of causal understanding of the natural order and of the identification of things, nor the discourse of moral and prudential requirements. They are classically employed in commenting on the surfaces and on the look of things, and particularly on the look and surfaces of people: on their physiognomy and on the outward expression of inner states in faces and bodies and voices. Examples of such impressionistic predicates applied to a person's movements are: clumsy, stiff, delicate, tense, agitated, rough, gentle, deft, feeble, stately, hesitant, cringing, languid, tentative. Every reader will be able to add many more English adjectives to the list, and there will be many more impressionistic adjectives applying to the quality of a movement or of a face in other languages. Impressionistic and physiognomic predicates are the least translatable of all predicates, and they have to be learnt by long familiarity with diverse contexts, leading to a direct grasp or intuition of the analogies implied. Impressionistic predicates are happily applied not only to persons, but to landscapes, cities, and streets, to works of art of all kinds, to animals, and to any living thing. When we have not deliberately adopted the stance of a scientific observer, we bestow our emotional responses on the persons and objects seen and heard, as if we are in a dialogue with the external world. We have to make an effort, the effort of scientific objectivity, to separate perception from evaluation, to be aware only of the measurable properties, and not the good or bad expressions, on the face of things. We have to make an effort to see the colour of someone's eyes rather than the expression of friendliness or hostility in them.

One is driven in moral philosophy to think first in abstract terms of good and bad, right and wrong, and of justice, because the logical and epistemological problems have in history arisen at this abstract level. But one may present a wrong picture of morality, and of its place in human life, with these abstract notions alone. Two qualifications at least have to be added: that moral distinctions are woven into our everyday perceptions of the world; and that, in a natural spoken language such as English, there exists a great variety of predicates in common use, about which it would be misleading firmly to assert, or firmly to deny, that they are properly to be called moral predicates. Whether a particular predicate is to be called a moral predicate often cannot be determined except by reference to a conception of the good within which that particular quality has some moral significance. The larger and more variegated our vocabulary of impressionistic description is, the better able we are to explain to ourselves and to others why we admire and love the particular persons and activities which we cling to, and why we have come, through our perceptions, to form the particular conception of the good that we have. Hume's fact-value dichotomy, when applied to our perceptions of persons, activities, places, robs the external world of its affective qualities. Phrases in music and in speech no longer have their expressive shape, colours no longer harshly clash, and there is not a directly perceived, and objectively real, difference between a dull and deadening symmetry and a beautiful symmetry, when we look across the park and up to the facade of the house. Even in a narrowly moral context, when a person's courage in a period of persecution and stress is assessed, and when he reflects on his own conduct and on what he must not do and must not say, the perceived manner and spirit of his behaviour, the impressions that he makes on those around him, are often as morally significant as the bare actions barely recorded in a value-free narrative of the events.

To summarise: Hume's ghost, still haunting the corridors of the learned, may be put to rest by reflection on two propositions about the settled use of language by the unlearned:

1. The grounds for calling things which are X's good X's are logically dependent, for many types of X, on the grounds for classifying things as X's. This is a conspicuous bridge on which we can pass from fact to value and back again: from identification to evaluation and back again.

2. The all-important words "ought" and "must" have a common logic in all their uses, whatever kind of possibility and ne-

cessity is under discussion—moral, prudential (means to ends), epistemic, or nomic. When we use the modal forms ("ought", "must", "may", "might", "can", "could") in moral contexts, we are talking about possibilities qualified as good or bad, better or worse. The "good" and "bad" applied to possibilities express particular conceptions of the good, associated with diverse ways of life; and these conceptions are matters of opinion, defensible by argument and more or less coherent. There are also great evils which befall men and women and which are independent of any particular conception of the good and which arise from the basic needs of living creatures. One can produce arguments to suggest, though not to prove, that the fanatic who advocates the massacre of infidels has a warped and evil conception of the good. But it is not similarly a matter of disputed opinion, requiring argumentative support, that murder, like pain and starvation, considered by itself, is a great evil to be avoided, within any way of life.

Kinds of Possibility

⁋ In support of the second proposition a story can supply three extra-linguistic contexts, or situations, which will differentiate three types of judgment conveyed by the same sentence, each with the presuppositions attached which differentiate any one type from the other two. A look-out man and a get-away driver are sitting in a car outside a factory which their mates are burgling. The look-out man says to the driver, "They ought to be leaving the factory now." He may intend a judgment of epistemic necessity, modified from "must be leaving now" to the weaker "ought to be leaving now", with the attached presupposition of the known regularities not being cancelled by any abnormal features of the situation. The judgment is empirical in the sense that only known facts of common experience are relevant to its evaluation. But it is semantically complex, in the sense that the judgment is not to be matched immediately with some observed phenomenon. A massive background of knowledge of normal regularities has to be presupposed before it can be evaluated. It is a modified judgment of epistemic necessity, because it implicitly asserts a probability: "In all probability they are leaving the factory now."

Alternatively the speaker may intend a prudential judgment, which is of the kind that Kant distinguished from moral judgments, and which presupposes normal human propensities, such as not wanting to be caught and punished. This is also an empirical, but semantically complex, judgment, not permitting direct comparison of the judgment with the observed fact. The driver might concur with "That's true: he ought", or more weakly, with "That's reasonable: you are probably right that he ought to leave now." The third possibility is that the speaker intends a moral judgment. The burglars ought to be leaving the factory now, because they gave an undertaking not to linger and not to endanger the look-out and the driver, and consequently they have an obligation to leave. Clearly there could be a rational argument about whether the undertaking is an overriding, or sufficient, reason for endorsing the moral judgment in the particular circumstances, and different conceptions of the good could enter into the argument, which might prevent an agreed evaluation. But anyone who objected "Why is the endangering of the undertaking a reason at all?" would be refusing to enter into the domain of moral discourse; he would be like the sceptic who questions the presupposition of the usual regularities in evaluating the first two judgments.

Consider another type of situation in which judgments of necessity and both theoretical and practical possibility become urgent and important, a type of situation to which poetry and fiction are always returning: the situation of retrospection and regret. Any person's actual history can be seen in retrospect as a track between two margins. Just over the left margin are all those things that could or might have happened to him, and that nearly happened to him, stretching back along the margin into the past. On the right-hand side of the track are all those things that he might have done, and that he nearly did, and that were real possibilities or options for him, stretching back into the past. He may, looking back, regret what might have been, seeing another possible life for himself, regretting the sudden turns of fortune, as in Machiavelli's representations, at the same time as he regrets the choices that he failed to make, the other possible life that he might have made for himself. This last is the regret that Eugene Onegin felt. A person may make moral judgments of many different kinds about the past: that he ought to have chosen differently at various junctures; or that he did not deserve the reversals of fortune that he suffered; or that he ought to have foreseen some of the worst outcomes; or that the history, taken together with the possibilities alongside it, shows him repeating a constant pattern in his personal relations, which he ought to acknowledge to himself; or that he has wasted opportunities of correcting injustice; or that he probably has done as well in helping his family and his friends as in retrospect seems to have been possible, and that therefore he has less to regret than he had thought: and these are just some specimens of moral reflection, as everyone to some extent experiences it, being aware of his present desires and feelings, and of his present situation, as indissolubly tied to his past good and bad fortune and to his past good and bad decisions.

He explains himself to himself by his history, but by the history as accompanied by unrealised possibilities on both sides of the track of actual events. His individual nature, and the quality of his life, do not depend only on the bare log-book of events and actions. His character and the quality of his experience emerge in the possibilities that were real possibilities for him, which he considered and rejected for some reason or other. From the moral point of view, it is even a significant fact about him as a person that a certain possibility, which might have occurred to him as a possibility, never actually did occur to him. In self-examination one may press these inquiries into possibilities very far, and this pressure upon possibility belongs to the essence of moral reflection.

Historical explanation, both as practised by historians and in moral or prudential reflection, is differentiated from standard forms of scientific explanation by this invocation of the real and singular possibilities which shadow the actual events. It is always a matter of judgment for the historian to decide what the real possibilities were. At every stage of the story there were near-misses, might-have-beens, live options that were vivid at the time but that are now eclipsed by the actuality. Good historians, and true and just personal reflection, restore the plural possibilities of the particular juncture with such vividness as to highlight the felt contingency of the actual events, as they were experienced at the time. The first aim of a good narrative historian is to narrow the possibilities between which a choice was made by excluding the possibilities that were not present to the agent's mind, and that he could not be expected to recognise. The precise opposite is required in deliberation about the future: the requirement of rationality is imaginatively to multiply the possibilities that are present to one's mind.

I am stressing the logic of singular possibilities because they make up the environment in which moral judgment and reflection typically occur. Not alone among eighteenth-century moralists, Hume represents moral thought as principally the activity of projecting upon reality adjectives of approval or disapproval, as commentary on, and criticism of, human performances. Once again the model of Newton misled all those who aspired to be the Newton of the moral sciences, observing human nature as Newton had observed the starry heavens above. Thought about practical, emotional, and moral concerns is principally a matter of dangling a cluster of singular hypothetical propositions before the mind's eye, some empirical and some evaluative and some mixed: looking back to possible pasts, because we can see that the possibilities really existed, and also as guidance to possible futures.

The second reason for stressing the place of singular possibilities in moral concerns is that they largely determine our conceptions of the good, in so far as we form and change our conceptions of the good in the course of our lives and as the result of our experience. Conceptions of the good are normally fairly, open to change in the light of experience, and they are normally composed, like a mosaic, of many distinct interests and commitments, usually exhibiting some general pattern, but probably not a very clear one. Having accepted some possibilities marked as open to us within our culture and in our circumstances, and having experienced the consequent disappointments, we continually revise our conception of the worthwhile possibilities: sometimes even to the extent of rejecting the circumscribed possibilities of our own culture, and turning the track of our life through a right angle in a moral conversion. Because Hume assumes the standpoint of an observer of humanity when he describes and explains moral discourse, his moral philosophy has a profoundly conservative tendency; it is as if his Toryism was built into his epistemology. For Hume the essence of morality is to be traced in the in-built regularities of human sympathy and of concern for general happiness, sentiments always rewarding and reliable. To represent morality as a concern for so far unrealised, and inadequately imagined, possibilities is to reverse this conservative picture. As new possibilities arise from social and technological changes and are realised, more new possibilities are incidentally imagined, but not in any discernible order or predictably.

It is important to moral theory, and to the concept of the conception of the good, that moral conversions are far from abnormal; there are moral theories, such as Hume's and Aristotle's and also some forms of moral relativism, which imply that they are abnormal. Such theories must be mistaken. They imply that a person's conception of the good typically and normally has a stability, based upon habit, which precludes any sudden illumination, as of Paul on the road to Damascus. The truth seems to be that many people in many cultures do cling to stable conceptions of the good, reinforced by experience, while for others, and in richer and more mobile societies, an abrupt change of moral concern is always possible. One might at any time open up for consideration possibilities which were remote from the margins of one's previous life. This is the equivalent in private life of the great "premature" reformers in public life who exposed radical new possibilities of political or social action, as the early Christians did, or as early feminists did, or as Gandhi did with civil disobedience and non-violence.

Conceptions of the good are normally the outcome of a person's experiences of satisfaction and disappointment, of the personal influences in his life, of his temperament and his talents and his imagination, and of the habits prevailing around him, rather than of original thought and abstract speculation. Under the heading of "temperament" are included all the associations stored in the unconscious mind. This is how a particular conception of the good first starts to develop, before it is later refined, defended, justified, and further developed by reflection. If she is a reflective person, she reflects on her experience with a view to opening up better possibilities for the future, within the limits set by her talents and dispositions, as she sees them. When a person is thinking about moral values, she is always thinking about the limits of possibility, limits set both by natural causes and by a past history which is not too deterministically interpreted; rather the history is seen as a series of might-have-beens running parallel with the actual events and the actual decisions. Prominent among the limits of possibility, circumscribing a person's conduct and experience, is the limited power of the imagination to envisage an improved way of life with different commitments and purposes, which, once concretely envisaged, might be judged to be altogether better. Alongside the possibilities which were wrongly ignored, as it seems in retrospect, and the possibilities which one retrospectively recommends ("I ought to have done it"), there are the possibilities towards which one has (as it were) an optative attitude—"If only (or would that) I had been a more generous person." A wish to have, or to have had, a different nature, and to have been in this sense a different person, is often a highly moralised attitude, and the past can be its object as well as the future.

In the representation of human lives, and in making the unrealised possibilities in them as vivid and as real as possible, fiction in all its forms has an advantage in comparison with history. Historians, apt to be mesmerised by the discovered facts and by their apparent sequence, look for causes which may make the sequence seem comfortably intelligible. But in fiction, that is, in drama from ancient times until the present and in modern novels, the tension of unrealised possibilities—"Will she or will she not?" as in Richardson—can be preserved just because the actual fate of the hero or heroine does not monopolise and dominate attention, being itself only an invention. So in following an imaginative story on stage or in a novel, we recapture the sense of uncertainty and of open possibilities which we experience in actual living. We are introduced by the author to the missed possibilities on the margins of the actual events supposed, because dramatists can create their own space of possibilities, as painters create their own space within a picture. As Aristotle remarked in the *Poetics,* the poet, unlike the historian, focusses attention on what might happen in the general run of human affairs, rather than on the bare facts. Reading or hearing his story, we are not worried by the thought of unknown particular causes and effects, at that time and at that place, as the historian is, left alone with his counterfactual speculations. That is why drama, and in modern times the novel, are the necessary arts of the moralist; they are "more philosophical and more serious", in Aristotle's words, than history. They survey and illustrate the range of human possibilities beyond the mere known facts.

Good and Evil Again

❡ An objector will now say: "Your rejection of Humean subjectivism has as one of its supports the Aristotelian account of predications of good, namely, that good is predicated by analogy in different categories and with different natural kinds and with different kinds of artefact. But you have been writing about the great evils of suffering, the destruction of life, starvation, without explaining how 'good' and 'evil' are used in these other contexts. This is apparently not a use of 'good' which fits into the account of predication by analogy. 'Good' and 'evil' are here being used in an absolute and detached sense. Does not the Humean analysis, the so-called subjective analysis in terms of the speaker's attitude and sentiment, apply to this range of value judgments?" Replying to this, I do not deny that there are two distinct uses of "good", distinct in grammar, sometimes distinguished as the attributive ("a good so-and-so") and the predicative ("It is a good thing that so-and-so"), and that it makes sense to speak of happiness, freedom, and pleasure as good things, as contrasted with unhappiness, imprisonment, enslavement, and pain as bad things: states to be pursued for their own sake and states to be prevented and avoided for their own sake. For such states there is no need to appeal to any distinctive conception of the human good, although a distinctive conception of the human good would be invoked when a decision had to be made in some situation between these evils, giving priority to the avoidance of one over the avoidance of another.

I have argued that the states universally accounted bad and to be avoided and prevented have a clear priority in practical thinking and morality. When one is identifying ends of action that are common to all humanity, one thinks first of the great natural and man-made disasters, against which both prudence and morality are required as protection and as shields. There is no tolerable life, decent and worth living, without some protection against the evils just listed, and this protection has to be supplied by the social and political order, as well as by the prudence and the moral judgment of individuals. The great evils are those states of affairs which are to be avoided for reasons that are independent of any reflective thought and of any specific conception of evil. Physical suffering, starvation, imprisonment, the destruction of one's family or home, are felt as great evils by anyone in virtue of being a living creature with all the needs that are common to living creatures. If one sees a chained dog released and allowed to run free over the grass, one sees an image of freedom and an illustration of the evil of constraint. In so far as the great evils are man-made, as in a tyranny's domination by killing, imprisonment, and enslavement, they are so far great moral evils, although the Communist leader, or the Grand Inquisitor, will refer to his own conception of the good as redeeming the evil.

Procedural Justice: A Summary

❦ In the earlier books of the *Republic,* and before the philosophical education of the Guardians is described, Plato presents justice as the proper ordering of distinct and complementary roles and functions both in society and within the soul. It is there taken for granted that warriors and thinkers, merchants and peasants, have specific goals, and therefore specific virtues depending on their distinct goals and functions. Justice is for Plato the co-ordinating and stabilising virtue. Hume, in common with other British moralists of his century, envisages both an actual and a desirable convergence of all humanity on shared moral sentiments, admitting local varieties around a common centre. He is not greatly interested in the specific virtues attached to specific social roles and functions. In this respect he is to be ranked with Kant as sharing the Enlightenment programme: that humanity should be united across all barriers of social status and origin in shared moral concerns and values. Benevolence and a capacity for sympathy were to be the primary virtues and they were appropriate in every rank of society and to every office and function.

The arguments of this book are throughout directed against this Enlightenment conception of a single substantial morality, including a conception of the good and of human virtue, as being the bond that unites humanity in universal sentiments or in universal moral beliefs. Humanity is united in the recognition of the great evils which render life scarcely bearable, and which underdetermine any specific way of life and any specific conception of the good and of the essential virtues. The glory of humanity is in the diversity and originality of its positive aspirations and different ways of life, and the only universal and positive moral requirement is the application of procedural justice and fairness to the handling of moral conflicts between them.

Substantial conceptions of justice and fairness are evidently involved in the distribution of absolute goods and in the avoidance of evils. These conceptions of substantial distributive justice, as opposed to procedural justice, are derived from particular conceptions of the good. Under what conditions, if any, is it just that a person should be punished by loss of life, or by the infliction of physical pain? Is an assassination always an unjust act, even the assassination of a tyrant? These, and countless other questions, are questions of substantial justice, and convergence on universal agreement is not to be expected. Universal agreement can be expected, in the name of rationality, only on the methods of fair argument which will arbitrate between the different answers to these questions, when an answer is needed for public purposes and social arrangements.

So great has been the influence within contemporary moral philosophy of Hume, Kant, and the utilitarians that it has been possible to forget that for centuries the warrior and the priest, the landowner and the peasant, the merchant and the craftsman, the bishop and the monk, the clerk who lives by his learning and the musician or poet who lives by his performances, have coexisted in society with sharply distinct dispositions and virtues, as we see them recorded in stained glass or in stone or in memoirs and histories. Varied social roles and functions, each with its typical virtues and its peculiar obligations, have been the normal situation in most societies throughout history. More specifically, there has always in Europe been the contrast between the statesman-warrior and the priest; and within Christianity the virtues of this world have been set against the virtues that fit the eternal world, pride and splendour against humility and austerity. People have always needed to rationalise these contrasts within conventional morality by allotting to each conventionally demarcated type distinctive virtues and distinctive obligations. The Christian churches, and Christian societies in general, accepted without too many qualms the distinct roles and obligations of monarch and subject, and of master and servant. As in Plato's *Republic,* justice was to be found in a *concordia ordinum,* in a balance and harmony between the classes of persons in society, each fulfilling distinct functions and responding to distinct obligations within a stable and coherent whole.

In opposition both to Plato on one side and to Hume on the other, I am representing procedural justice as regulating the necessary conflict between chosen roles, with their attached obligations, and not as a means of making these roles coherent within an accepted and overarching whole. Justice is a means of enabling them to co-exist in civil society and, as far as possible, to survive, without any substantial reconciliation between them, and without a search for a common ground. It is neither possible nor desirable that the mutually hostile conceptions of the good should be melted down to form a single and agreed conception of the human good. A machinery of arbitration is needed, and this machinery has to be established by negotiation. Justice can then clear the path to recognition of untidy and temporary compromises between incompatible visions of a better way of life.

Hume's Last Reply

❡ Hume's ghost must produce a last defiant reply, which takes this form: "You have argued that statements asserting necessities ('oughts' and 'musts') all have a common logic, whether they assert natural necessities, moral necessities, or epistemic necessities. I had claimed that all statements asserting necessities, as contrasted with unmodified categorical statements, represent only the motions of the judging mind, and not objective relationships in the external world: different movements of the mind for natural necessities and for moral necessities. You substitute presuppositions for movements of the judging mind, different presuppositions for natural necessities and for moral necessities. What have you gained by this substitution, over and above a change in terminology? We both seem to be agreeing that the idea of necessity, as I call it, issues from the judging mind and that it does not correspond to anything observed in nature. This was my point, which you prefer to make in logico-linguistic terms and I in a psychological vocabulary."

My reply is: "The gain from the substitution is that my account explains the type of reasoning that surrounds and supports assertions of moral necessity as well as assertions of natural necessity. In the *Treatise of Human Nature* and in the *Enquiry concerning the Principles of Morals* you left the impression that there can be no reasoning worthy of the name in the discussion of moral problems and of the ends of action, and that the final appeal must always be to the sentiments which nature has implanted in us. Your followers in our century have gone even further than you in insisting on the great difference between reasoning about causal necessities, which are matters of fact, and value judgments, which only express feelings and sentiments: not only are the two types of judgment entirely different in respect of their claim to rationality, but no valid inference can pass from one type to the other, according to you and to them. Against these two theses of yours, I argue that the singular counterfactual judgments about causes and effects in history, or in our own lives, or in public inquiries into accidents and civil damages, and in many other types of empirical inquiry into necessities and possibilities, employ reasoning that is typically no less and no more determinate and objective than moral reasoning, which is just a species of practical reasoning. In addition, I claim that there can be valid inference from empirical judgments to evaluative and prescriptive judgments, and vice versa, for the reasons which Aristotle originally supplied. Certainly I agree that there is a clear distinction, which ought not to be blurred, between empirical judgments about natural necessities and causes on the one side and moral prescriptions and moral evaluations. They arise from very different situations: a scientific investigation or a historian's study or a court of inquiry on the one side, and a deliberative council or a moral exhortation on the other side."

4

Individuality and Memory

❡ We know now, as a lesson of recent history, that those theorists who have in the past represented respect for justice as a necessary and universal requirement of any morality were right. If this barrier against the drive to domination, and against overwhelming ambition is subverted, we are in a moral desert, where there are no limits and nothing is forbidden in the pursuit of power. We have learnt that education and culture, scholarship and science, are paper barriers, which generally, and with a few exceptions, collapse more easily than the philosophers of the Enlightenment could have imagined. This is because education and culture are scarcely barriers at all. Their function is to open up possibilities and not to close them down, which is the effect of justice as a virtue. Precisely because a conception of the good, that is, of the best activity and enjoyment for human beings, is positive and specific, it is divisive. To acquire and to exercise the dispositions and the skills that make a person effective and useful in government entails not possessing certain dispositions and skills which are pre-eminently necessary in the pursuit of other conceptions of the good—for instance, in the patient concentration on single problems in science and in scholarship, or in the attainment of absolute precision and accuracy. The art of government, like the art of music or of poetry or of mathematical invention, is one respected art among others, each of which requires innate and acquired gifts peculiar to itself.

This is just one reason among others why there is no such thing as the single good for man, defined as the best activity for all human beings to aim at, irrespective of the innate differences between them and irrespective of the differences between their ways of life. But everyone can reasonably be asked to respect principles of fairness and justice in negotiation and compromise. Arguments are therefore needed to show at the same time that the minimum conception of justice is a universal moral requirement, and that no specific conception of the good can ever be a universal requirement. The arguments ought to show that the two aspects of morality are in some respects complementary and that they form a common structure, each leaning on the other. The argument turns upon the notion of individuality.

Memory and Variety

❡ Among the distinguishing features of humanity, such as possessing native languages quickly learnt, mathematics slowly learnt, legal systems, poetry and the arts, is the habit of dwelling upon the past: of recalling the past and investigating it with motives unconnected with prediction of the future. Intelligent but non-human animals learn from the past and from their past they acquire associations which they use in controlling their behaviour. But there is no evidence that they either do or could cause their minds to linger among memories, or to cherish and to preserve their memories merely as memories, as a person might preserve photographs merely because they represent the past. Photographs are part of the furniture of the external world; my memories are mine alone, the stuff of my inner life, even though I may choose to communicate them to others in some form or other. My memories, conscious or unconscious, preserve the continuity of my experience and they confer some unity and singularity on my life as a whole. Not even identical twins have the same memories, because of differences of perspective and of the accidents of location. Most of us have a multitude of memories which we know to be ours and no one else's.

A sense of one's own singularity is sometimes called a sense of identity. When a person thinks of himself as different from everyone else because he has had experiences which no one else has had, then it is probably better to say that he is thinking of his singularity. The identity of an individual includes his singularity, his being different from everyone else, but the scope and emphasis of the concept is different, because it implies also the continuity of his existence, which justifies, for instance, his having one name applicable throughout his existence. If a person seemed to alternate between existence and non-existence, his identity would be in doubt, and he would be singular on each occasion. Stevenson's Jekyll and Hyde should certainly have suffered from an identity crisis, if they had had time to think of it, because of the discontinuities in their experience. But neither Jekyll nor Hyde had reasons, as the story goes, to doubt his singularity, the uniqueness of his distinct personality and of his memories. The notion of individuality includes the idea of being singular, or in relevant respects unique, and also of having a definite identity, that is, of having an appropriately continuous history—appropriate, that is, to the species to which the individual belongs.

A moral interest in individuality is to be contrasted with philosophies, such as Aristotle's, which represent moral education as designed to produce the ideal specimen of humanity, having all or most of the excellences that are peculiar to the species. Such a philosophy introduces the notions of completeness and of perfection, of the requirement that no essential virtue missing in a complete life, notions criticised in Chapter 1. An alternative aim of moral education is to develop a single second-order disposition and ability: the ability of a person to work out for herself, in the light of her own experience, a specific picture of the best and most praiseworthy way of life which is accessible to her and which, more than any other, engages her imagination and her emotions. Most people, uninfluenced by philosophy, will not think of their moral purposes in such abstract terms as "the best way of life". They are generally committed to some relatively concrete aim, or set of aims, more or less vaguely envisaged: perhaps the happiness of their immediate family, some particular achievement in an art or sport, some political achievement, some particular service to their community, some service to God as they conceive it, or some combination of these. But they can properly be said to have a specific conception of the good if they are prepared, after reflection, seriously to defend and to justify their way of life, to themselves and to others, as being more than the way of life which they happen unreflectively to have chosen for themselves, or which they happen to have inherited. They genuinely believe, and they are prepared to argue, that their overriding concerns are the concerns that ought to guide their conduct, even if, because of weakness, they do not always, or even generally, do so.

Their arguments in defence of their overriding concerns in some cases do, and in some cases do not, involve them in legislating for humanity as a whole. Some overriding concerns, when fully and explicitly analysed, amount to programmes ideally to be followed by all men and women, carrying with them a universal imperative. If a person's overriding concern is the realisation in his life of the main Christian virtues, then he will usually be concerned that all other people, or at least all those who have access to Christian teaching, should show in their actions this same overriding concern. But if a person's overriding concern is the perfection, as far as possible, of a particular craft or art or method of inquiry, and if he is prepared to argue, after reflection, that this concern leads him to the best and most praiseworthy activity of which he is capable, then he will not be concerned, and will not argue, that all other people should share his overriding concern. When he argues that his striving for a peculiar perfection in a very limited domain is the best activity of which he is capable, he may invoke some more abstract moral purpose. The abstract moral justification might be found in the artistic striving itself, or in the value of art to humanity, or in the exercise of imagination, or in some combination of these. None of these reasons for calling his artistic efforts the best activity of which he is capable entail that all mankind should have the same overriding concern. Unlike the concerned Christian, and unlike a convinced utilitarian moralist, and unlike a Kantian moralist, he is not legislating for humanity when he forms, explicitly or implicitly, his own conception of the good. He will argue only that his conception of the good is defensible and coherent, not that it is mandatory.

There is one universal moral requirement that touches conceptions of the good: the higher-order requirement that every person should have formed through experience some conception of the good, which is her overriding concern, and which she is ready seriously to defend. Obviously she may not be the kind of person who would ever put her conception of the good into words in some distinct formula. Her conception may show itself only in the duties and obligations that she recognises, and in the virtues to which she attaches the most importance, and, most of all, in the considerations which she cites where her moral opinions are challenged. The overriding concern for the good may be simple, or it may be a complex set of distinct concerns, not all of which are closely related to each other. The universal requirement associated with conceptions of the good is that every adult person should have some authentic and defensible commitment, which engages her strongest feelings and which guides her actions.

Conventional morality's emphasis on the value of an individual life, as opposed to the life and survival of a species of animal or plant, is traceable to the presumed singularity of persons, each of whom possesses a character and style that is peculiarly theirs, and this individual essence is destroyed when the individual is destroyed, and the world is to that degree impoverished. The loss is absolute, even when the person killed, or allowed to die, happened not to be an admirable human being. One does not normally think that the disappearance from the world of a horse, or even of a cat, is necessarily a serious loss, if the disappearance is considered by itself and without regard to its effects. This is not,

I think, just a prejudice, sometimes called speciesism, a loyalty to one's own kind. There is a reasonable argument behind it, and this is the argument from singularity.

But what is the singularity of persons, the individual essence, the something lost in death, not present in animals, who must not be allowed to suffer, but whose mere death is not by itself an evil? One plausible answer is just that every person has the potentiality of forming his own conception of the good, even if not everyone realises this potentiality. Some people simply imitate others and drift indifferently and without commitment or passion throughout their lives. J. S. Mill argued that the progress of mankind, in generating new possibilities of happiness, depends on the diversity of "experiments in living", and that increases in general happiness depend on the absence of conformity and conventionality. Idiosyncrasy, and diversity in conceptions of possible values, contribute to the general advancement. Mill remained enough of a utilitarian to take increases in general happiness as self-evidently the supreme end of human endeavour; but he encouraged variety in specifying the enjoyments and activities which would in the long run most effectively contribute to this end.

I have been arguing that the diversity in conceptions of the good is an irreducible diversity, not only because no sufficient reasons have been given, and could ever be given, for taking one end, such as the general happiness or the exercise of reason, as the single supreme end; but also because the capacity to develop idiosyncrasies of style and of imagination, and to form specific conceptions of the good, is the salient and peculiar capacity of human beings among other animals. This is their nature, as it is also their nature to speak a great variety of natural languages. It is also their nature to understand logic and mathematics and to respond emotionally to the ideas of fairness in negotiation and of procedural justice, even though they may differ in the specific conceptions that they attach to these ideas. The universal necessity of respect for the negative virtue of fairness is a consequence of the diversity of conceptions of the good. Basic fairness in negotiation and in swapping concessions are requirements that prepare the ground for a shared negative morality independent of specific conceptions of the good: this is the common decency, which moral and religious fanatics try to undermine in the name of their particular conception of substantial justice, derived from their particular conception of the good. The great evil is the destruction of respect for generally recognised fair procedures of adjudicating and compromising, procedures which have been built up over time out of earlier recognised procedures, and which are always capable of being reformed. Just as theoretical reason, being a species-wide and cross-cultural endowment, is at home with logic and mathematics, practical reason, as a species-wide and cross-cultural endowment, is at home with the weighing of alternatives, with judgment and with compromise.

Individuals and History

❡ The mutual dependence that binds the universal, negative aspect of morality, protection against evil, to the diversity of ends and beliefs still leaves the value of individuality unexplained. There is one principal and evident respect in which each person is singular and sharply differentiated from all other persons: each person has a unique history. Apart from personal histories there are biochemical differences in physical make-up which can be used to single out one person from all others: biochemical fingerprinting. This is obviously an interesting contingent feature of human beings. But it is a feature which has only fairly recently been recognised and understood. That each person has a unique history has always been known, because it is a necessary truth. If we decide that Stevenson's Jekyll and Hyde were two persons, and not one unusually changeable person, then each had a unique history that was discontinuous, with inexplicable gaps; the gaps constitute a strong reason for not considering them as two persons. If we decide that there was one inexplicably changeable person, then he has the normal single history, with singularly abrupt changes of character and personality. Confusions of identity, and split personalities with secluded memories, do not constitute sufficient reasons for denying that to each identifiable person a singular and distinct history is attributable, even if it is an anomalous and interrupted history. If I am told that the last Dalai Lama is the same Dalai Lama as his predecessor, I may agree; but I shall still insist that he is not the same person, if he does not have the same singular and distinct history. I am presupposing the usual European concept of a person, which constructs a criterion of identity from a story of spatio-temporal continuity in conjunction with some continuity of memory. This concept is built into prevailing moral beliefs in the West, including the belief that the person who is punished for the crime must be one and the same person as the person who committed the crime.

One might suggest that the sequence of experiences in the life of a person does not differ in any relevant respect from the sequence of episodes in the life of an animal; this would imply that earlier experiences enter into typical causal explanations of later experiences, but that there is no closer link between the elements in the sequence than this causal one. This is an implausible suggestion, if only because of the power that language gives persons to reflect upon their past, to recall it deliberately and to make mistakes in recalling it, to be over-attached emotionally to some parts of their past, or conversely to struggle to keep them out of mind and not to think of them. So dense and heavy are memories in the human mind, sustained by reflection and by description in a language, that some philosophers, conspicuous among them Bergson, have claimed that the memory-relationship constitutes the dividing-line between two categories of being, mental things and material things. Not only is it true that the sequence of a person's past experiences is peculiar to her and is peculiarly hers, but it is also true that the accumulation of her memories, conscious and unconscious, of her past experiences is peculiar to her. No one else remembers and recalls exactly what she recalls, when she chooses. Her memories are her possession and her property, a kind of spiritual capital, and the income from it, in the form of reviewed experience, is merged with the incoming experiences of her continuing life in the present.

Memory is so dominant and pervasive in our lives that it is virtually impossible to write about it except in metaphors. Literal descriptions can single out one kind of memory as opposed to another, deliberate calling to mind, for example, as opposed to unconscious or pre-conscious storing of past experiences. But the immense, sprawling phenomenon in its entirety, constituting the largest part of our inner life, is apt to be encompassed only by the kind of metaphors that Bergson unashamedly used. These metaphors have to convey the unmechanical and confused connections which intimately link our memories, conscious and unconscious, to each other and which "colour" all our later experiences and which form the constantly changing and enriched "background" to later experience: metaphor again. Our memories do not constitute an aggregate, which can be compared to a heap of stones, in Leibniz's image. They can be better compared to another kind of aggregate, a compost heap, in which all the organic elements, one after another as they are added, interpenetrate each other and help to form a mixture in which the original ingredients are scarcely distinguishable, each ingredient being at least modified, even transformed, by later ingredients. This comparison is intended to run counter to the famous implications of the association of ideas as presented by Hume and other British empiricists. The associated ideas were represented as mental atoms which preserved their identity and integrity unmodified by their neighbours in the chain of association; they attract each other when charged by repeated and recurrent continuities, but they remain distinct like beads on a string. The opposing hypothesis or opposing description invokes Heraclitean and William Jamesian metaphors of rivers and streams, which represent our memories fusing with each other to form our consciousness of our own past experience—immediate, middle distant, and distant past: my continuous inner experience, the world as it presents itself to me but not to anyone else.

Opposing hypothesis or opposing description? I am sure that the theory of the association of ideas, taken as a theory of our relation to our own past experiences, is a misconception, and that the contrary theory fits the phenomena, as we know them, vastly better. When I delve into my own past, and try to recapture an experience of mine, I know that I normally arrive at a picture of the past which is confused, overlaid by accretions, often emotionally toned, whether the picture is in words, or is a visual image, or more commonly is a mixture of the two. Never do I have an experience of discreteness, of Hume's "separate existences". It is reasonable to speculate about the reasons for the comparative lack of discreteness in human memory and for its unmechanical properties, the tendency of our memories to interpenetrate. From the point of view of natural history, what is the advantage of this apparently holistic device which is installed in the human brain for preserving links to the past? One may guess that probably the capacity to learn quickly to speak and to understand a natural language depends upon a memory that works holistically and not mechanically, and not by the association of ideas, as in classical learning theory. Most of a child's learning of her native language involves memories of the speech of others, memories which are unconscious and unnoticed. At all stages of her learning, both elementary and advanced, her knowledge needs to form a holistic system rather than a simple atomistic one: that is, the associative links between sentences and contexts need to form a network of many elements mutually and repeatedly interacting, and not in a one-to-one mechanical and linear relationship. Otherwise the rapidly acquired innovative capacity to fit previously unencountered sentence forms into new contexts, and to adapt sentence forms appropriately, is not easily explained. This speed in language learning suggests that complex networking is at work in a child's memory. In addition, the classical association of ideas does not plausibly explain the phenomenon of "take-off" in language learning; there is a critical accumulation of memory of words, sentences, and contexts which is sufficient to produce a sudden leap forwards in understanding and use, a mastery of a section of the language for the first time. It is as if a sufficient multiplicity of sentence-types and context-types have been activated simultaneously for the first time, and a network established.

These are speculations to suggest why human minds, preserving a relation to the past through their own history, might be expected to work holistically, and not as a machine memory works. It has so far proved impossible for machines to come near to the flexibility and resourcefulness of human language-users in adaptation to new linguistic contexts and to new situations. Apart from the mastery of a native language, many of our dispositions and capacities seem to form themselves by analogous processes of holistic accumulation, whereby a person by stages in her development acquires a character and an everyday style, and a set of physiognomic and expressive properties, which are distinctive and, when fitted together, seem to others peculiarly her own. This is not a surprising fact, given that her stored experiences form an immensely complex network of interacting associations, a network that will not be duplicated in all its particularities in any other mind. It is reasonable to expect that each person should develop, on the foundation of a singular genetic endowment, idiosyncrasies of style and manner which are peculiar to him, so peculiar as to enable his friends to identify him with certainty through many disguises: a tone of voice, a style of walking and running, a laugh and a smile peculiar to him, a distinctive handwriting, peculiarities of facial expression, a look in the eyes, a choice of words that is characteristic of him. These are just a few of the obvious features of personality which are the outward expression of an inner nature, the nature of an individual, formed by a biological inheritance continuously and untraceably modified by experience and by memory. That the sources of individuality are untraceable, and that we cannot in fact understand a person as a composition of influences, help to explain the value attached to individuality. If we thought that it might in principle be possible to reproduce the individual character and style of a person by re-combining the elements, we should naturally begin to lose the sense of absolutely irrecoverable loss when a person dies.

The philosophical question is: Why do we in fact attach so much value to the individuality and singularity characteristic of human beings? Ought this singularity to be cultivated and expressed, rather than repressed in the interests of normality, the attainment of a species-wide ideal of complete humanity? There are two kinds of answer to these questions, two interpretations of the "why." The first set of answers point to observable facts of human nature, evident in history and in introspection. The second set of answers supply reasons why we ought to cultivate and to express individuality, both in the interest of individuals and also in the interests of humanity in general and of our descendants: the second set of reasons therefore are arguments for the value of individuality, alongside the value of procedural justice, as one of two fundamental and invariant elements in the very various conceptions of the good which are defensible.

Facts of natural history and of natural sentiments go a long way to explain the value of individuality: particularly sexual love and sexual attraction, and, derivatively, the varieties of friendship and of insight into the minds of other persons. Erotic feeling has to single out a person from a population, and the feeling has to be both excited and sustained by the perceived and imagined psycho-physical peculiarities of the person, peculiarities that are the outward expression of an inner essence. The inner essence has to be penetrated and known in an apparent, partial, and temporary overcoming of the separateness of persons. Erotic feeling that does not become concentrated on an individual, but rather is drawn towards any specimen of a type, seems a weaker feeling, because diffused: also weaker because it is more easily explained in causal terms, or at least more open to explanation, less immediate, and less unpredictable. Throughout Western literature and in Western philosophy, from Plato onwards, sexual love has been associated with the desire to know an individual person with a peculiarly violent curiosity, which becomes a desire to enter into another inner world, and to take possession for a time of another person's consciousness through the body that expresses that consciousness. The object of desire is the embodied soul of a singular person coming to the surface in an individual style of moving and standing and looking and talking. The imagination of the lover is set in motion by the particularities and distinguishing features of the person loved.

Imagination

❡ "Imagination" is the word that cannot be avoided in this context. The elaboration of erotic feeling is always a work of imagination and not of reason and of argument. One does not love for a reason, any more than one enjoys a joke for a reason: the particularity of the occasion excludes calculation and causal analysis, or makes them irrelevant. Unconscious memories and past associations, perhaps also some conscious memories, unpredictably come together and are focussed on the peculiarities of one person, and release the imaginative energy of sexual love. In weaker forms this energy of imagination necessarily enters into all our knowledge of friends and of other persons. We see them as embodiments of feelings to which we must try to respond. We see their physiognomy rather than their anatomy, their expressions rather than their measurements. We have to imagine their feelings, mimic for ourselves the peculiarities of their individual styles and manners, and respond to their gestures. So we may love not only persons, but individual places: particular rooms, landscapes, streets, houses, for reasons which we cannot explain and with a transferred force of imagination. Places seem to match or to echo, at least for a time, some buried memory of a possible and unrealised happiness, which might perhaps have existed in a dream rather than actually realised in a strong attachment. Sexual love seems the bedrock, biologically necessary, original case of the power of the imagination, and the cultivation and elaboration of sexual love in all its varieties is the work of culture as much as of nature. The elaboration is unique to human beings. It is unhistorical, and contrary to experience, a Manichean error, to think of erotic feeling as comparable with hunger and thirst, as a primitive need, as rationalist philosophers often have suggested. We all feel hunger in more or less the same way, but our sexual desires and practices vividly express individual natures as well as something of the customs of a particular culture. They are penetrated by thought, by symbolism and by imagery, and therefore by that kind of thought which is called imagination.

The raw material of intellect is argument, and argument proceeds by general rules, generally acknowledged. The leaps and swerves of a person's imagination do not follow any standardised routes, and the thought that follows a standardised path would not be called imagination, just as the thought that does not advance by rule-guided steps would not be called intellect. Why particular visual patterns, natural scenes, melodic forms, historical or religious themes, classical myths, characters and plots in drama, arouse in a person a peculiar emotional response is usually unknown to him and almost always unknowable by anyone else. In the typical case there are no salient reasons to be picked out, except of the most vague kind, and there are no sufficiently distinct causes to be dug out of the person's history and memories. A strongly imaginative response draws upon an immense accumulation of interacting memories and associations, layer upon layer combining and re-combining.

Freud's concept of condensation, applied by him to dream thought, is useful and suggestive in this different context. So much of a person's unconsciously remembered past may be revived by particular images or formal structures that it is impossible to point to single experiences, or even to sets of experiences, as the identifiable causes of the response. In cases where the imaginative response is especially strong, there will be no direct, traceable path from a set of original experiences to the highly specific visual or musical forms to which the person responds. Nor will there be any evident and generalisable relation between any set of experiences and the specific forms which convey this effect to the person's imagination. The memories involved are too many, too confused and too blurred by their past interactions, probably extending into the person's childhood, beyond the range of conscious recall and analysis. The vast capacity and scope of the art of Shakespeare or of Titian create a space into which a great variety of fused memories can enter: suggestions of happiness, of loss, of transience, of love, of innocence, and of old age. Into these inchoate and unparticularised suggestions, as into a vast, unfurnished cave, each person insinuates some highly specific version of these indefinite themes, which he finds sharply realised in the specific forms of the works before him.

Sexual feeling, in the variety of its expressions in different individuals, illustrates the complexity of the condensed memories which form a person's imagination. The naturally preferred sexual practices of different persons, and their sexual peculiarities, do not show some straightforward and easily understood correlation with past experiences and family situations. Highly individualised fantasies intervene, enriched by images peculiar to the individual, and the tempting generalisations from typical family situations to typical sexual dispositions generally fail. Personal histories do not exhibit this kind of regularity: each person carries not a mere log-book of experiences, but rather a selective interpretation of the past, which both forms the person's needs and also serves them once they are formed.

To think of the imagination only in association with the creation and enjoyment of art and with erotic feeling is plainly wrong. Every sufficiently intense thought that is concentrated in particularities and that evokes some strong feeling is an exercise of imagination. Here a philosophical claim most boldly expressed by Marcel Proust in *A la recherche du temps perdu* has to be considered, a claim that inspires that entire work. Proust argued for two propositions: first, that the value that we attach to works of art, and also the value that we attach to sexual love, arises from the fact that both are embodiments of one person's unrepeatable and peculiar sensibility, the first in a permanent, and permanently valuable, form, and the latter in a necessarily transient, and ultimately unsatisfying, form. The second proposition was: all persons have the possibility of grasping the essence of their own sensibility, and of recapturing the peculiarities of their own buried experiences from their past, if only they realised that they had this potentiality. If only they would cultivate this unstructured kind of self-knowledge and would try to recapture their past in some concrete form, they would liberate the formative power of their peculiar sensibilities; and this is their only safe route to a realisation of happiness. Every person possesses the very same power that a genuine artist has fostered and realised by a lifetime's dedicated work.

Like most philosophical or religious plans for salvation and secure happiness, Proust's plan requires a conversion away from the way of the world and from its illusions, from the treadmill of social success and from the vanity of human wishes. We have been deceived, both in our lives and in the criticism of art and literature, by a conventional and superficial picture of the self. The true and singular self of each individual is buried below the reach of introspection and of conscious attention. With effort and dedication it can be brought into the light of imagination, if and only if we probe into the original sources of our more inexplicable and irrational feelings, however improbable and accidental the sources may seem. A deadening incrustation of conventional classifications of human concerns, and of human powers, prevents us from looking inwards and from recognising the unnamed exaltations and depressions of our inner life for what they are, the revelations of our real nature, concealed by our social role. Instead of trying to conform to generalised and established models of human distinction, of standardised intelligence and of approved tastes, we should strive to extract and to express the singular responses of our own sensibility and of our unique perceptions. We know the responses to be an authentic disclosure of our own true nature when they are associated with an emotional force which cannot be explained by any reasonable calculation. There is a loss and a waste, which can never be repaired, if we lead our lives always facing outwards towards the shared and commonplace business of the world, and always turning our backs on the intimate emotions and perceptions, which are our own peculiar contributions to the sum of human experience.

Proust's theory of the true self was applied by him principally to the enjoyment and the creation of art and of literature, and to love in all its forms: but the theory itself has a wider range. Proust distinguished between the enjoyment of art by the connoisseur and man of good taste, who cultivates a comparatively superficial enjoyment of the historical patina and decorative features of any work, as contrasted with the true enjoyment of art, which requires penetration to the singular essence of a particular artist's or writer's vision, a vision that distinguishes him from every other artist or writer whom he superficially resembles. The only style that is in the long run interesting is a highly personal style, a revelation of a nervous system and of a slanted vision, which together light up a dark face of reality from an unpredictable point of view: not the style, so pleasing to the critic Sainte-Beuve, which is dominant at a particular period of history, burying the different individuals behind the common fashion.

The Proustian theory of the true self becomes a more general moral theory in the context of a casuistical problem familiar in both world wars. Is it ever justifiable and right to set at risk the lives of soldiers in order to save from destruction great works of art and to preserve them for posterity? Is it ever justifiable and right to incur a certain loss of life among a few soldiers for the same reason? Proust's own answer to both questions is a clear no. He is rejecting the false aestheticism, as he conceives it to be, of the dilettante and of "les célibataires de l'art", who revere the object rather than the spirit or soul which animates the object and which finally constitutes its meaning and its value. The great cathedrals of France, which were subject to bombardment, embody the work and vision of countless individual masons and wood-carvers in the Middle Ages, of architects and engineers, of artificers in many kinds of material. The persistent work and the individual vision of these forgotten men are the soul of any cathedral, considered as a work of art rather than as a building dedicated to God. The sum of their individual visions and of their work issued in the beauty realised in the building, and when we are moved by the beauty we are moved by the human achievement, both the beauty and the achievement being peculiar to this building. To take another example: the deliberate loss of human lives in preserving for posterity a single work, for instance, Vermeer's *View of Delft,* could not be justified, because the value of this most beautiful painting, of the actual physical object, resides in the lifelong work and thought, and solitary dedication, of Vermeer; it resides in the imagination of that unique person, elaborating his own singular vision of what painting might be as a representation of reality. If the physical object had been destroyed, the spiritual value residing in that individual's dedicated labour and vision would not have been destroyed; but posterity would forever have lost direct access to this extraordinary human being and to his unique discoveries in painting. Posterity ought not to be in the position of having purchased access by the expenditure of the lives of other human beings, since the sovereign value of individuality is the immaterial value which is embodied in the painting itself. Every truly original work of art is a monument to the irreplaceable potentiality of individuals and to the singularity of their imaginative visions. We cannot reasonably sacrifice individual persons, as if they were replaceable objects, in defence of works of art.

This is a rather obscure argument; and I am far from sure that I represent Proust correctly. In spite of the obscurity, the argument seems to me to reflect correctly the intuitions that many persons do have in reflecting on this particular casuistical problem, provided that they have not been misled by philosophical arguments into accepting some consequentialist theory of ethics. The deliberately incurred loss of a soldier's life in war is often a justifiable means to an end, if the loss contributes to the defence of justice against injustice. Justice has to be defended if individuals are to retain their independence and their power to form their own lives. The ends-means calculation is therefore not unreasonable in this case, as it is in the other. Nothing is mechanical and unfeeling in the work that made the cathedral, and it would be a mechanical and unfeeling calculation that would lead to the death of a number of soldiers for the sake of the future aesthetic pleasure that the building would continue to provide. Only if individual persons offered to risk their lives to protect the building would individuality have been respected. Otherwise one falls into an error similar to that of staging a fraudulent and unjust trial in order to convict someone of fraud and injustice.

A person's history, consciously and unconsciously remembered, has twisted her imagination, which has been starved at some points and over-developed at others. Certain rhythms and shapes and landscapes are intensely significant for her; others, which are normally accounted beautiful or beneficent, are for her inert. There is no reasonable requirement that she should twist herself back, against the grain, towards some imposed normality of concerns and interests. On the contrary: if one takes the standpoint of humanity as a whole, and not of the individual, there is no call for the repetition of a type, not even of an ideally balanced type of human being. A culture is built by the piling of individual testimony on individual testimony in a long tradition. There are myriads of different crafts, skills, enjoyments, and professions which may stimulate a person's imagination, each of which has its history within a particular culture. Working in the garden, skiing down a slope, climbing a mountain, designing an experiment in a laboratory, suddenly seeing a connection in philosophy, drinking and talking with friends, watching children and grandchildren play, buying a first house, returning to a childhood home—in each of these activities some people will find their imaginations fully engaged, to the surprise of other people who might find the very same activity deathly and stultifying.

Transcendence

❡ In the peculiar workings of their individual imaginations during these activities, men and women may even arrive at a sense of transcendence, a kind of epiphany, in which they seem to themselves to have escaped for a time from the usual limits of possible experience, and to have alighted on a privileged moment that takes them outside their ordinary and confined routines. In moments of transcendence we feel free from the lapse of time. Proust in his novel describes several such experiences of transcendence. Some sight or sound in the present calls up, in a moment of intense emotion, a buried experience from the past and brings it into the present, overcoming the desolate opposition between past and present, and giving the subject a sense of a timeless reality in the inner world of his experience, a world untainted by categorisation and description. Behind the conventional, public history of successive events, there is the true, primitive experience of one's own imaginative insights, dependent upon the peculiar distortions of emotion which are one's own, if only one will attend to these twisted visions, and if only one will do the work that is needed to convey them in some appropriate medium. This is the work of bearing witness, and of bringing testimony, to one's own sharply biassed experience of life, and of conveying to one's descendants an authentic and abnormal perception of that which most makes life seem worth living, beyond the transient enjoyments and predictable disappointments of everyday experience. A return to normality, away from attachments to the past, is a return to sterility; every population of intelligent persons should be a patchwork of minorities in the pursuit of deviant conceptions of the good, held together by a shared respect for fairness.

That the experience of transcendence has always been recognised cannot be doubted, because of its place in so many kinds of literature: in association with religious mysticism, with aesthetic experience, with erotic experience, with nature mysticism, and with isolated perceptions and epiphanies of the kind that Proust and Joyce and many poets have described. Accident plays an essential part in descriptions of transcendence and in its sources in imagination. The experience that carries a person beyond the successive routines of experience is initiated suddenly and unpredictably. It is a visitation, and it carries its own authority. Chance and unpredictability are essential to the authority of the imagination, which has always been associated, from Greek literature onwards, with such concepts as the demonic, the inspired, the possessed. The most interesting and profound solutions in art or science, it is thought, are hit upon by accident, or, if there is a cause, it is a trivial causal factor, or a casual occasion, that triggers the solution. So love and happiness, at their most intense, often seem to have come into existence by accident, by a chance collocation of events, or by a trivial coincidence of causes. The openness of the imagination, coming from the uncontrolled interactions of unconscious memory, always leaves a margin of the unplanned and the unexpected. However carefully a person deliberates, in Aristotelian style, about the ends of action, assessing what most makes life seem worth living, he ought always to be open to surprises, discoveries, and uncertainties. Through an accident of experience he may discover in himself a disposition that he had never believed that he could have, or he may find a deep significance, and a source of enlightenment, in an activity which he had thought was trivial and worthless. We cannot know *a priori* what is superficial and what is profound from the standpoint of the developed and free imagination.

Many people have undergone, in a leap of the imagination, a moral conversion, entirely changing their beliefs about slavery, or poverty, or the status of women, or the treatment of prisoners, or the right to die, or about sexual promiscuity, or patriotism, or war. The imaginative leap of a moral conversion is still open to the control of rational assessment, which entails argument and counter-argument. But a chance event might have been a necessary step in leading to a new, and more defensible, conception of justice, for this person and at that time. There is a limit to the argumentative control of conceptions of the good, for the same reason that there is a limit, as argued by Kant in *The Critique of Judgment,* to the control that an artist's talent should exercise over the unexplained and unplanned discoveries of his genius, when he transcends the "academic" and the "mechanical" elements in his thought.

Virtue and Justice

❡ Courage, a capacity for love and friendship, a disposition to be fair and just, good judgment in practical and political affairs, a creative imagination, generosity, sensibility: these are all dispositions and capacities which are grounds for praising and admiring men and women. But we know, from experience and from history, that the following propositions are true:

1. Differing social orders, and different historical circumstances, promote and constrain different versions and conceptions of these abstractly named virtues.

2. Because of their personal history and memories, different admirable individuals can never attain to some of these virtues, at least in any normal version of them, and are strongly inclined to others.

3. Some of these virtues are incompatible with others in all known and foreseeable circumstances of human life.

4. It is a general truth about human nature that the greatest, most admired, and most praiseworthy human beings are often those who developed one or two of these abstractly described cardinal virtues to the highest degree, while altogether lacking others of them. It is also a general truth that some societies have specialised in the cultivation of some of these virtues, or in the cultivation of some version of them, to the total exclusion of others. Lopsidedness is a fact of human history and therefore a fact of human nature.

Some individuals and some cultures have formed a moral ideal of the complete person combining all or most of the virtues in an ideal balance. I have argued that this particular conception of the good is only one among indefinitely many possible conceptions of the good, and that it certainly does not constitute the foundation of morality. Morality, like knowledge, does not have a single, clear foundation. Most people realise that their own moral beliefs and attitudes, and also the beliefs prevailing in the community to which they belong, are one set among many. With this realisation they encounter a problem which all humanity, at every stage of development, always has encountered. This is the permanent problem of the infidels, the outsiders, the barbarians from across the frontier of civilised values as we conceive them; some just harmless infidels, some truly dangerous.

Because everyone comes, sooner or later in life, to at least one moral frontier, every morality has to develop a concept of justice to meet this problem. What is fair and just conduct towards those whose behaviour is an outrage in the light of our conception of the good? There are two routes to an answer: the first, the more usual in moral philosophies of the past, derives a conception of justice from an already established conception of the good. So just conduct towards the infidel, perhaps involving the Inquisition, has been explained as a reasonable consequence of the Church's doctrines of salvation. Within a Rousseauesque, or Jacobin, society, the conception of the good embodied in the notions of the general will and the common good justifies forcing men and women to be free, in a sense of "freedom" which they do not themselves accept as a moral ideal. Rousseau's solution is a modern form of the classical solution, coming from Plato and the Christian churches: abolish the frontier, create a new solidarity, leading to a new unanimity. This is the solution by moral conquest, if not physical conquest. The second route avoids conquest by recognising that justice is not one virtue among others, but rather it is the independent pre-condition of any of the various conceptions of the good being realised.

There is evidently no way of rigorously proving, by an *a priori* argument, that there is an incoherence in not recognising procedural justice as a virtue that is independent of every conception of the good. One can only present the reasons that make it seem reasonable to see morality as having two interdependent aspects rather than as the seamless whole of Aristotelians and of natural law theorists, of utilitarians, Kantians, and deontologists. That conceptions of the good are, and ought to be, divergent and often conflicting; that the peculiar value of human life lies in the individuality of the person, of her perceptions and imagination—these are reasons, briefly summarised.

The Dual Aspect of Morality

❡ There is another type of consideration which may supply a motive for accepting this dual aspect theory of morality, even if the motive cannot be described as a reason which any rational person must of necessity accept as a reason. Through most of history several of the dominant religions of the world have had, as part of their creed, the belief that they are destined in the long run to triumph over the infidels. It has been part of their creed that they must be on the winning side, even if winning, in some religions and sects, has an entirely other-worldly sense. When secularism and religious scepticism spread in Europe, and mankind was to be saved and to recapture innocence through revolutionary politics rather than through the churches, Jacobins and Communists inherited the conviction that their triumph over their enemies in the long run was built into the nature of things. The slaughter-house of history will be finally redeemed when one true morality—Christian, Jacobin, Communist—reigns everywhere and all heresies and deviations are suppressed. One might without injustice add to this list the enlightened, progressive liberal, follower perhaps of Condorcet and J. S. Mill, whose creed included a picture of the soul which guaranteed that the rational methods employed in the natural sciences would step by step undermine supernatural enthusiasms and credulous fanaticisms in all the corners of the world. The experimental spirit would lead to a utilitarian morality, concerned only with the spread of human happiness, which in turn depends on the free enterprise of individuals. Happiness and freedom to experiment will everywhere be recognised as the conquering values of the modern world.

But suppose the Enlightenment picture of the human soul,

with reason still on top and still sure to triumph, is no more realistic than its predecessors: suppose that the power of the imagination, and of its attachment through unconscious memories to the past, is far stronger than had been believed, both for good and for ill. Then the secular and liberal philosophy of history will prove as illusory as all the other philosophies of history which preceded it. If so, a safeguard against fanaticism and wars must be found outside the historical process and the teleologies that are imputed to it.

Justice and Pluralism

❦ Can a thin, procedural concept of justice have an imaginative power in the minds of people, more powerful than the appeals to freedom, familiar in the rhetoric of nationalism and tribalism all over the world? This is not strictly a philosophical question and it is not a clearly answerable one. On a philosophical level I can only indicate how this might be possible. The first step is to bring the concept of procedural justice into relation with pictures of human variety, and the second step is to understand human variety through the study of history and of language. The path for the imagination to travel, if its destination is the procedural concept of justice, is through a great museum that displays a long succession of aesthetic ideals, mutually influencing each other. Some ideals are strictly individual products of a personal style, some impersonal but products of a very definite culture persisting over centuries. They are all inexhaustibly complex and subject to many different interpretations; some are so remote from us here and now as to be virtually unintelligible. It is certainly possible to understand, and to re-create in one's own mind, the emotion aroused in the eighteenth and nineteenth centuries by conceptions of the unity of mankind, as in Condorcet and in Saint-Simon and in Michelet. It is possible also to understand the excitement that was aroused in Europe by the thought that one belonged to a party, or to a philosophical school, which was about to unify mankind for the first time, as Hegelians and

Marxists and positivists thought. But there is a contrary excitement that comes from the study of history and from aesthetic experience, when aesthetic experience is set free from philosophical systems. It might be called the Herodotean pleasure, the excitement that comes from travel across frontiers in both time and space. So many peculiar ways of life, so unlike the programmes of animals and of thinking machines, so many defiances of biological constraints. The last thing that one wants, as one leaves a museum, is some imperialistic takeover of the art and of the languages of comparatively weak, and perhaps comparatively inefficient, societies which preserve a way of life, a language, and a means of expression which are peculiarly theirs and which perhaps have a long history.

Respect for minimum procedural justice and respect for the study of history are naturally tied together. Arguments in negotiation turn on precedents and the comparison of cases in their historical setting. All adjudication calls on history. At another and deeper level there is the truth best expressed by Hume and Burke: that a long and continuous history, the survival through vicissitudes, of an institution, of a language, of a community of people living together with shared conventions, by itself earns respect; fair treatment of them requires that their long history, and their mere survival, constitute a special claim to respect. Men and women normally find reassurance and consolation when they can identify themselves as parts of, and as participating in, a long and continuous history. As in some forms of transcendence, they see a victory over transience and triviality. They find a moral interest in celebrations of the past that link ancestors to descendants, an interest that is partly gratitude for an inheritance and partly a sense of belonging to an order and to a future.

Within a museum the objects in the Egyptian rooms are not in competition with the objects in the Greek rooms and the Mexican rooms. They are pursuing different ideals. Similarly any admirable person has some intelligible conception of the good, even if, like Rimbaud, he is a great poet driven by his rage and his genius to extremes of injustice in his behaviour towards others. Rimbaud obeyed moral imperatives in his pursuit of his authentic vocation, but these would not be duties and obligations recognised by anyone who lacked his vocation. It is an error and a distortion to grade human beings on some universal scale of human virtue as more or less admirable, more or less praiseworthy, as if they were pointed by God or nature towards some single target, which was Aristotle's metaphor. The exercise of imagination in pursuit of the private good calls for more than toleration: it calls for the encouragement of individuality as an absolute value.

It is only fair that those whose imaginations and reflective emotions respond principally to ancient traditions, and to the way of life of their ancestors, and who believe after reflection in the supreme value of local attachments and of loyalty to their own people, should not be morally harassed, just because they think it wrong to reject conventional morality for the sake of some highly individual conception of the good. The traditionalists have formed their own conception of the good, and it may be both reflective and also authentically rooted in their perceptions. It is required of them only that they should be reasonably fair in their attitudes towards those radicals and practising individualists who have a contrary conception of the good. Their duty is to participate in an institution which adjudicates between competing claims in accordance with recognised rules of procedure. This actually happens when in a pluralist society a nation-state comes into existence in which tribes or sects with incompatible ways of life accept a common legal or parliamentary tradition. Of course this often fails to happen.

Of people living together in the same society with completely different conceptions of the good and of the best way of life, it is sometimes said that arguments between them must come to a dead stop, an ultimate sticking-point. This is not true either as a matter of logic or as a matter of experience. The supporting arguments for a conception of the good are not normally to be expressed as linear deductions from ultimate premises: they normally invoke a variety of metaphysical, historical, and psychological beliefs, alongside records of individual feelings and imaginative experiences.

It does not follow from the proposition that the duties that support procedural justice and fairness are absolute, in the sense that they are not relative to particular conceptions of the good, that they therefore always override other duties in all conceivable circumstances. That is why "in all normal circumstances" has to be added when the rules and principles of procedural justice are compared with traditional notions of sovereignty. There may be circumstances in which it is justifiable to behave unjustly—for instance, in order to save human life, or to defeat an incipient tyranny which would clearly lead to greater injustice. There may be circumstances in which the injustice is minor, and the evil to be averted is so great that the injustice is justifiable. These are casuistical problems which cannot be settled *a priori*. Here it is necessary only to explain what "absolute" is intended to mean in this context. An absolute duty is a duty which is not to be derived from any person's conception of the best life, but is a duty for everyone, whatever ends he or she may be pursuing. It is a duty that arises directly from a combination of two virtually universal conditions of human life: first, that men and women need to live together in societies and states of some kind, and, second, that all men and women both do, and ought to, encounter persons with contrary moral concerns and with incompatible conceptions of the good, both beyond the actual frontiers of their societies and within them.

There is an important difference between justice as a universal virtue and the disposition to love and friendship as a universal virtue. The duties that arise under the heading of minimum justice are definite and moderately specific. They are the specific duties of observing the procedures of fair discussion, negotiation, adjudication, and compromise that prevail in a society, unless one has reasonably rejected these procedures as being in themselves unjust and unfair. Black men and women in contemporary South Africa can and do fairly reject all the restraints imposed on them in the name of the local conception of justice, on the grounds that the minimum decencies of procedural justice are not available to them. The unfairness of a procedure is established by the same rough tests as the unfairness of a particular employment of the procedure: Are the moral claims fully presented? Do the interested parties have reasonable access? Is there genuine argument and counter-argument? Are precedents, if any, respected? Are the rules of procedure reasonably consistent and known? Is the procedure free from threats of physical force? Whenever we are thinking of the duties that everywhere support the virtue of justice, we are thinking of the risk of domination, expressed in the settlement of moral issues by the threat of force or by conquest.

Hobbes, and most theorists in the social-contract tradition, misidentify the central problem of morality when they ask under what conditions persons can reasonably be expected to live together given that they have conflicting appetites and interests, and given that they have a drive to dominate in order to satisfy their appetites. In spite of the influence of Thucydides on Hobbes, this picture of the soul comes from human mechanics, not from the evidence of human history. History largely consists of the intersecting histories of competing religions, competing languages and customs, competing cultures, competing conceptions of the good, competing systems of government. There is every reason to hope that history will continue to show moral and aesthetic diversity and competition, as humanity develops new sciences, new styles of expression, new conceptions of the good, new ways of life. Ferocious appetites and interests are more easily reconciled by rational calculations within a society than ferocious conceptions of the good and of right and wrong. No games theory, no ingenious mechanisms of rational choice, can help in moral conflicts as they might with competing appetites and interests. No appeals to a possible unanimity and to a possible sentimental harmony, as in Rousseau, have proved to be plausible. No project of unanimity by conquest and take-over, as in Hegel and Marx, is either plausible or morally acceptable. No doctrine of universal human rights can convincingly be represented as independent of a particular, historically traceable conception of the good and of the freedom of the individual as a primary good. There have been languages in which moral arguments have been conducted, into which the notion of human rights could be translated only with difficulty. On the other hand the notion of justice is embedded in an unavoidable and transhistorical predicament: the necessity of agreement by discussion, without conquest or outright surrender, on regular procedures for negotiating with hostile neighbours who have different conceptions of the good. Justice grows, and winds its ways, out of this common soil of an inevitable predicament, and then, as it grows in any one place, it is twisted into various shapes as it comes into contact with different conceptions of the good and different ways of life. Recourse to violence and conquest would be defensible as a just course of action when it could be shown to be the only way to resist an evidently greater injustice.

Justice and Liberal Assumptions

❡ John Rawls's account in *A Theory of Justice* defines justice only as this concept is used in a liberal and democratic society. The concept so defined does not accord with the intuitions of a very conservative population, or of any social group which is primarily influenced in its social morality by ideas of tradition, particularly by religious traditions and sacraments, or by historical myths, or by the authority of a church, or by the supposed intrinsic value of inherited customs and conventions. Can the minimum procedural conception of justice as a universal moral requirement, independent of any conception of the primary goods, also be accused of presupposing the acceptance of liberal values, such as the autonomy of the individual? Is not this moral requirement to negotiate, to argue, to submit to adjudication under open and known procedures, whenever there is a conflict of ends, either within a population or at its borders, an essentially liberal requirement? Can it ever become a universal moral requirement, equally acceptable to authoritarian moralists who are guided by the supernatural claims of their church or sect, and to conservative moralists who respect the obligations and way of life of their own social group, and are indifferent, or hostile, to any foreign ways of life? I am claiming universality for the requirement because of the universality of the predicament which gives rise to it: authoritarian and conservative moralists, recognising that humanity after the expulsion from the Garden of Eden and from the paradise of original harmony will always produce infidels and moral outsiders, will be driven to the policy of conquering and dominating them in a totalitarian state, unless they establish agreed-upon and precedent-following procedures of negotiation.

The criteria of validity in a moral or legal argument cannot be altogether independent of the criteria of validity in the study of logic and mathematics. Practical reason, used in the procedures of moral, political, and legal argument, observes the species-wide rules of theoretical reasoning; but it adds some of its own, because it generally needs to end with a definite conclusion, and it cannot usually end with a suspended judgment. In practical matters, both of law and of morality, situations arise in which judgments have to be made without sufficient reason. In respect of rationality, argument around the table on matters of practical policy does not essentially differ from arguments, for example, among historians, lawyers, or scholars of literature and language, and in other imprecise inquiries, which are sometimes inconclusive.

But this still leaves open the question: does the concept of minimum justice presuppose the conceptions of the good which are dominant in a liberal society? Suppose a person claims that her church, through the valid orders of its pope, bishops, and priests, is the repository of moral truth which comes directly from God, and that the sacraments of the church, in the ritual of admission to the priesthood and in the installation of bishops and of the pope, ensure that God's authority preserves moral truth through pope, bishop, and priest into the present time. Therefore she says that her morality, her conception of the good, leaves no place open for fair negotiations about institutions and prac- tices involving substantial moral concerns, as her faith defines them. So-called unfair means of forcing the infidel to act in ac- cordance with God's word are not only morally permissible, but even moral duties. The natural question to ask this person is: "What are the grounds for your belief, and for your assertion, that you have direct access through the church to God's declara- tion of moral truth? Is this a matter of historical evidence, or perhaps of some convergence of historical evidence and meta- physical argument?"

To this infidel challenge at least two kinds of reply may be made: the believer may completely separate truth from grounds of justified assertibility and from grounds of belief, and claim that, at least in moral contexts, there is no relation between the truth of an assertion and the grounds of evidence that would be cited in support of the assertion, if it were challenged. The knowledge of truth which is derived from a supernatural author- ity, in this case from God through the sacraments of his church, is knowledge quite independent of grounds and of evidence, in any ordinary sense of evidence, and independent of the kinds of argument that are required in non-theological contexts. The au- thority, supernatural in origin, is directly felt and directly recog- nised by the individual believer, and this feeling of the supernat- ural, occurring as part of the experience of an individual, is the only certification that there can be, and also the only certification that is needed, for fundamental moral truths. Either one accepts the existence of a supernatural order or one does not: but—on this view—the question is begged against the supernatural if one demands empirical evidence for the certification of supernatural authority. If supernatural authority in morality is an internally coherent possibility, then it is not unreasonable to expect that it should be revealed to an individual in a moment of grace and of illumination: particularly not unreasonable if at the same time heavy supporting stress is put on the fallibility and eternal in- completeness of human knowledge when it is the outcome of merely human calculations and reflections.

This is as near as I can get to a philosophy which rejects the moral requirement of fair procedures of adversary argument in enabling conflicting conceptions of the good to survive side by side. The second, less extreme defence of the rejection of procedural justice in the name of supernatural authority admits the relevance of grounds and of evidence in establishing that there actually is such a supernatural authority and that this authority has made known to us, through traceable channels, the true foundation of morality. This line of defence of an authoritarian morality leaves room for argument and counter-argument and for negotiation. Because there is the possibility of argument, there is the possibility of establishing fair procedures for authoritarians and non-authoritarians to negotiate and to arrange compromises; for instance, the non-authoritarians may be persuaded that, for the sake of justice, there must be provisions within the state education system for presenting the arguments that propose the infallibility of the church, in matters of faith and morals, presented alongside contrary arguments.

If one reconsiders the first defence of an authoritarian conception of the good, it is not immediately obvious why the minimum concept of justice should become part of authoritarians' morality, alongside their conception of the good. What is the argument which they must accept or ought to accept? If the authoritarian moralist totally rejects the requirements of evidence and of argument, and refuses to argue in support of this rejection, then it seems that the concept of minimum justice will have no grip on him. Argument itself, and practical reason, seem to him otiose in all serious problems in the conduct of life; they have their place only in narrowly prudential, legal, and technical questions of no great moral concern.

I will not have recourse to a transcendental argument, to the effect that such a position is incoherent. Rather my claim is, first, that it is a position which is for practical reasons very difficult to sustain consistently, and, second, that it is an unusual position, at least among European authoritarians and religious apologists. The authoritarian is in effect claiming direct supernatural illumination on serious moral questions, an illumination that is self-certifying and that other persons, not illuminated, ought to respect for no good reasons that can be offered to them as an argument. It must be noted that this is not the creed of a philosophical individualist, who claims his own imaginative conception of the good which he believes confers duties on him but not on other persons who have not had his illumination. Such an individualist is not so far prevented from sharing fair procedures of negotiation with others. He is not debarred from defending his imaginative conception of the good, nor from making it intelligible to those who do not share his conception. The difficult attitude to sustain in practice is that of the fanatic who requires other persons to observe duties and obligations, and to develop specific virtues, without providing them with any reasons for abandoning their previous conceptions of the good in favour of his supernaturally inspired conception. A man of faith, and of faith alone, who does not see this requirement as unreasonable and as unfair, can share institutions, and live at peace in the same city, only with fellow believers in a stagnant and holy society from which doubters and infidels are excluded.

Attachment to the Past

❡ The disturbing aspects of moral experience are not to be found in the common meeting-ground of procedural justice. For many persons in the twentieth century, and also in earlier cultures, they come from emotional attachments to the past and to the re-creation of the past and to its redemption from failures and betrayals. There exist duties and obligations that arise from personal and local loyalties, and from past commitments to a cause—perhaps to one which is now failing, and which has become an object of memory rather than of hope. There are obligations which are entirely backward-looking and which would not be explained and defended by any clear form of practical reasoning: debts of honour, either to persons or to groups and to societies who have had a certain weight and influence in one's life. The obligation might be more sensitively seen not as the repayment of a debt, but as the acknowledgment, much later, of a gift and of a contribution. The obligation in part depends on a particular perception of a past relationship. These obligations arise not from a common humanity, but from a particular history.

All through Shakespeare there runs the theme of betrayal, and more particularly of ingratitude, as a black evil infecting a whole life. Betrayal and ingratitude are indelible offences against the past, rendering it empty and senseless. The past is always apt to be lost, either by being unrecorded or disavowed or arbitrarily trimmed, like the edges of a photograph, or by having accident and chance removed from it and being turned into a moral story. Within many conceptions of the good, there is a loss in not recalling and celebrating whatever was good in the past, and an evil in ingratitude, a loss and an evil which are independent of any bad consequences in the future. It is a fundamental objection to any utilitarian morality that it looks only to future improvements to explain the duties and obligations of a person. The obligations of a utilitarian are to his descendants rather than to his ancestors. Those who have died, and who have thereby forever ceased to be sentient creatures, cannot for this reason impose any obligations on us, since it is alleged that only the capacity to feel gives rise to obligations and to duties.

This is not how most human beings in fact feel about their past and not how they ought to feel, if imagination and individuality are essential to human worth. The peculiar intensity of learning to speak and to understand one's native language, and of a very prolonged upbringing and dependency in a family, and the rituals attached to phases of maturity, all together establish an identity and a pattern. A person's intentions for the future conduct of her life often seem to her to be a development of the desires and aims which she can trace back to influences in her childhood, making sense of a long tract of time: as if she can see herself passing from preparation to a possession of powers and habits which at first she did not know that she could possess.

Not to feel gratitude towards the past is, within most conceptions of the good, a disabling defect, a kind of inhumanity; and a grateful disposition is a virtue, a form of generosity of feeling and the contrary of meanness and envy, the passions that surely destroy life and pleasure.

There exists in some men and women, as in Proust, a passionate desire to revive, to restore, and to repair the past in its full integrity, and to clear away deceptive representations of it. If this desire is felt at all, it carries with it a moral urgency to discover, or to re-create, the truth to experience concealed within a person's life. Truth to experience, an artist's and a poet's concern, is its own kind of truth, certified by the vividness and power of its expression. To those who have the mission to restore, it seems a form of cold ingratitude to leave the reality of a person's past life, or of an old institution, or of an artist's work, obscured by illusions. It seems a duty to bring the reality into the light again, and to prevent the efforts and the achievement from running into the sand and disappearing forever. Within this conception of the good, humanity as a whole, and each particular population, needs to bring to life, as far as is possible, the evidences of past vitality and to celebrate an authentic past, causing it to appear before our eyes out of its time. We do not study history principally as an exercise of practical reason or for the sake of the future. We study it, and we try to imagine the past, because these famous or strange things have been done by men and women, and there ought to be a monument.

Why is there this need of a monument? At this point conceptions of the good diverge again: for some thinkers preoccupied with time and with transience, the full recovery of some piece of past experience, and its re-entry into the present, provide a moment of transcendence and of exaltation, an escape from time. This was Proust's happiness, the recovery of the buried reality of a life. In a more widely shared conception of the good, illustrated in Shakespeare's sonnets and throughout literature, to keep a historical memory alive is to confer a kind of pagan immortality on a person and his acts. He will be placed somewhere in the vast museum of history, even if only in a corridor or in a dark corner. The further the persons and their deeds recede in time, the greater will be their dignity and the emotional response that they evoke. Everybody knows the power of old and discoloured photographs and of the remainders and relics which make a dead life, local and confined, swell into importance—as they do in a Hardy poem, or in the corners of an old house.

There is another kind of attachment to the past conveyed in literature and in art. The myth of the Garden of Eden expresses this attachment, and the myth of a Golden Age also. This particular sense of the past was fully expressed long before the didactic tone of the Romantic movement confused it. With some artificiality this attitude to the past, which is an emotion, can be analysed into a set of propositions. The essential propositions are: happiness is in the past and exists primarily as happiness recalled; innocence is in the past and has been lost irretrievably in the everyday contrivances of human existence; pure and unalloyed happiness depends upon innocence as its necessary condition, and a vivid image of innocence can produce a shadow, or a simulacrum, or a memory, of pure happiness. Innocence is to be understood as the reverse of worldly experience. Practical wisdom, the sovereign virtue in persons of experience who have lost their innocence, has no place in an imagined world of innocent persons. There is obviously no call for justice, either procedural or substantial, in a world of entirely innocent persons, where all purposes are transparent.

Why is pure and unalloyed happiness always in the past, and therefore an object of memory? The answer that suggests itself much too quickly is that pure happiness and innocence are to be found in childhood: the Wordsworthean answer, which seems to me superficial, a moralistic half-truth only. Rather, the imagined country of innocence is totally free from the strains of a perpetual contrivance of means to ends, which a person of experience and of practical wisdom masters. In the garden of innocence there is no activity of the kind which presents itself merely as work and as merely instrumental to something external to itself. Every activity is expressive of an impulse or interest or emotion which exists at the moment of action. The picture resembles Karl Marx's account of the state of humanity when the transition to Communism is complete: there is no longer any administration of persons, only the administration of things. There is no need of subordination, social status, government, law, or enforcement of justice, and nobody employs or manipulates any other person in pursuit of his own ends.

For the believer in the historical religions, innocence is to be found only in the afterlife, when the corruptions of experience in this world have been redeemed and cleaned away. For the political planners of the last century, who had secularised the Christian story of the Fall into a philosophy of history, the age of innocence was to be the outcome of the final social transformation. For most of humanity, whether or not they are believers in supernatural or historical redemption, innocence is something that they lost when they gradually discovered, as they grew up, that they need to plan, contrive, manipulate, to enter into drudgery, to divide their life into work and play, to accept social subordinations and barriers between persons, to accept the corruptions of wealth and the miseries of poverty; and, finally, to accept that enjoyment and happiness are always attained at a cost, and that it is not to be expected that pure happiness, happiness unalloyed, is attainable "in this world". Nature has not provided for it.

This discovery, and the attitude to experience which it engenders, have sometimes been called "alienation". I want to avoid this word because of its Hegelian associations. It is better called disappointment: it is the disappointment of natural hope. The survival of the species is probably assisted by instilled and persistent expectations, always to be disappointed. If human beings were born with a programmed anticipation of the limitations and disappointments of human life, they might be without aspiration; and they would not develop new moralities and new forms of social order without end, because they would not project their hopes and their disappointment, their sense that human life is perpetually out of joint, flat and discordant, into ideal forms which might reconcile them to the discordance.

If in every person's life there is this gradual accumulation of experience, the experience of dusty contrivance and of manoeuvre, the gradual loss of innocence, a growing knowledge of the narrow limits of happiness, and of fulfilment, then he or she will naturally look backwards across the experience to the early years of hope—"before I knew". It is as if one might revive the hope, and temporarily obliterate the intervening experience, if one recalled the past innocence intensely enough. One has the sense of being cut off, by the wear and tear of everyday business, from the hope which set one's activities in motion in the first place. One has to look back for the renewal of impulse, and one selectively recalls the past in the process. This is a mechanism that can most clearly be seen on the macroscopic scale, with nations and social groups. They renew their strength and their sense of their identity by returning to the myth of the noble ambitions associated with their foundation. This pattern of nationalistic thinking might be called the William Tell complex. Nationalism itself derives some of its energies from the mythical or quasi-historical reconstruction of an original innocence, before the complications of political experience began: as of the republican fathers of Roman greatness, or (in British Whig histories) of the yeomen of Britain meeting on the village green, or of the heroes and heroines of the Celtic twilight. Similarly in the lifetime of an individual the return in memory across the years of complication and contrivance to original hopes and expectations may produce new energies and perhaps even mitigate the feeling of irretrievable loss.

When Irish nationalism finally led to the establishment of the Irish Free State, complication, contrivance, compromise, and disillusionment unavoidably began. But even in these later years of the often bitter experience of political manoeuvring and compromise, it was always possible to revive the historical memory of the original, uncontriving Irish heroes buried in the Celtic twilight, and to derive some strength from imagining their simplicity, their directness of feeling, with their political actions flowing immediately from impulse. Similarly a person who feels himself to be tied down, for example, by the necessary mediocrity of professional life, by earning money and by civil responsibilities and by office routines, will try to reconstruct his original impulses. The golden promise of pure and unalloyed happiness will be abstracted in his memory from the mud of neutral and negative factors. Those who have had any experience of psycho-analysis know that it is too simple to represent the fantasies developed in childhood as causal factors that help to explain adult wishes and adult behaviour. It is also true that the fantasies associated with adult compromise formations help to explain a person's selective memories of his childhood. He sees the kind of impulses in his childhood which he wishes to see, because he needs to have this picture of his original simplicity if he is to persist with his present purposes through all the dreariness of calculation and of compromise.

For these reasons it is natural to associate a pure and unalloyed happiness with a golden past before we were, if not defeated, at least arrested and encumbered by experience. This image of an innocent past is immune to practical reasoning, and in the experience of individuals it is likely to be specified and expressed in a thousand different ways, as their memories edit their own past in accordance with their own needs. Persons' loves, friendships, loyalties, feelings of gratitude, their courage in persisting through difficulties in their chosen aims, are manifested in the obligations that they feel to be binding on them for reasons which may arise from their own memories and which are not felt by other persons. They must do certain things because of their memory of their original commitments before the disappointments of experience had begun. They would otherwise have lost the sense that their present way of life is authentically their own, and continuous with their past.

It may be worth adding that certain kinds of aesthetic enjoyment are very closely associated with this sense of unalloyed happiness irretrievably lost in experience. Attending to some perfect achievement in art, such as Mozart's *Figaro* or Casals's playing of Bach or a painting by Vermeer, very great pleasure may often be combined with an elegiac feeling, of sadness that perfect happiness is lost—that it is nowhere again to be found in the unimagined world and that it exists only in the perfect achievements of art. This elegiac feeling is very strongly associated with a high degree of formal perfection in art, as expressed in Keats's "Ode on a Grecian Urn". It is easy to understand that perfection of form, as realised only in certain kinds of art, may represent victory over the confusions and complexities of actual experience, and therefore it may represent a recovery of a happiness once hoped for, but known now to be unattainable in reality. Beauty has sometimes been interpreted as a promise of happiness, or more exactly, of a lost happiness.

Conflicts about Duty

❦ There are duties that arise from specific and substantial conceptions of justice which in their turn arise, directly or indirectly, from specific beliefs about the best way of life. The Grand Inquisitor may reasonably think of himself, because of his conception of the good, as fulfilling the duties of a just man as he burns heretics. In the most simple terms possible, what have I been saying to the Inquisitors, and to the opposing liberals, which ought to change their beliefs about their duties?

First, to the Inquisitors: "You are not absolutely evil, seeking conquest and domination for the sake of domination, rejecting any reasoned conception of the human good, like the Nazis. Your belief in forcible conversion as a duty follows from your conception of the good, and even when you want to be tolerant, you think you ought not to be, because you infer that it would be unjust—both to the faithful, who would be scandalised, and to the infidel who will go to Hell. You are ready to argue against liberals in support of your conception of the good and of the consequent substantial conception of justice. You can cite an array of evidence of the truth of your conceptions: not demonstrations, but evidence which you think a reflective person ought to find convincing. The liberal has exactly the same second-order belief about his own conceptions of substantial justice. My claim is that, given that you both assert an argued basis for your conceptions of justice and for the supporting duties, it is unjust and wrong to refuse to enter into an ordered negotiation about how you might live together with the minimum of harm, on each side, to the way of life which you consider the best. It is unfair to insist on having your own way.

"At the conclusion of the negotiation, if there is a conclusion, you will surely confront a conflict of duties, one duty following from your substantial conception of justice, as above, and the other duty following from the minimum and procedural concept of justice. One cannot prescribe *a priori* that in all conceivable circumstances you must prefer the duties of procedural justice over the duties of substantial justice as you conceive it. If your adversary in negotiation obstinately required you to sacrifice a number of the more essential features of the best way of life, as you see it, you might reasonably decide that this is morally impossible and that the cost of peaceful co-existence on an agreed and fair basis has been set unacceptably high. But it would be contrary to reason to refuse to abandon some less essential features of your preferred way of life in a reasonable exchange of concessions with your adversary. It would be unfair to require you, as a duty, to be on terms of close friendship with the liberals, or even to form a close community which includes them. You have a duty only to respect certain agreed rules and institutions of mutual restraint at points where your first-order moral concerns come into conflict. Injustice, according to the species-wide concept of justice, is the recourse to attempted conquest and domination when conceptions of the good come into conflict, even though fair and equal negotiation is still possible."

To the liberal free-thinker I say more or less the same: "In reaching a fair agreement for peaceful co-existence with authoritarian moralists, and with those with faith in supernatural revelations, and also with extremely conservative and traditional moralists, it is only fair that you should understand the distinctions on which they insist between the more and the less essential features of their chosen way of life. There are rituals and observances, particularly those involved in the upbringing of children, which seem to you, with your conception of the good, comparatively trivial and peripheral; but they may not be peripheral within other conceptions of the good. More generally, it would be unfair and unreasonable to extend the minimum concept of practical rationality, of fair discussion in public policy-making, so as to apply it to all important areas of human life.

"There have always been, and there will continue to be, conceptions of the good, and of the best way of life, in which the disposition to think and to be rational is not the supreme human virtue. For example, there is a conception of the good which makes the desire and ability to preserve one's own way of life, with its traditional duties and obligations, the supreme virtue, whatever this way of life may be. Within such a conservative conception of the good, rationality ceases to be an important moral concern. Another illiberal, or non-liberal, conception of the good simply identifies the way of life, and the virtues and duties, prescribed in certain inherited and sacred texts as the best way of life. I am assuming that there are arguments which support the alleged authority of the texts, and that these arguments are open to rational assessment. But the texts themselves are not; human criteria of rationality are allegedly out of place here. The minimum procedural concept of justice requires you to recognise and to understand these opposing conceptions of the good, and to be willing to enter into negotiation on fair and equal terms in order to establish institutions and customs which distribute frustrations of moral interests among the participants fairly and justly. To take the case of internal, not international, moral frontiers: it is likely that everyone, including you, will find some of the agreed-upon institutions and customs morally repugnant; but you will accept them because other features of your way of life have been left open to you in a fair exchange of concessions. You know that it would be unfair for you to insist on rationality, as you see it, being everywhere enthroned in the institutions of the society, including its educational institutions."

Conceptions of the Good: Nietzsche

❡ It would be contrary to the evidence of history to think of conceptions of the good as developing in isolation, uninfluenced by rival conceptions. Moral ideas cross and re-cross my imagined moral frontiers, sometimes finally obliterating them. It would also be unrealistic to suppose that either individuals or social groups normally act and conduct their lives in accordance with a coherent conception of the good, or that they have a clear and consistent picture of the best way of life, and of the reasons why it is best. People may arrive quite naturally at an eclectic position, in which they have come to respect duties and obligations which, if pressed, they would realise are drawn from different conceptions of the good.

One formidable sceptic still stands in the path that I am following, as Hume did earlier: Nietzsche. When so many of the claims of individuality have been admitted into the traditional shrines of moral theory, in this late age of individualism, is it not pathetic, says the Nietzschean, that you should still cling to this old moral vocabulary of "universal human predicament" and "absolute" duties, not relative to an individual aesthetic ideal? Cannot you finally let go of your prop, the last remnant of historical anxieties, and acknowledge that there is no such domain as that which the words "morality" and "ethics" purport to define? This fraudulent domain should be divided into a hundred pieces, of which some should be assigned for study to the biology of the race, and some assigned to aesthetic criticism and to the discrimination of individual styles. There will be no remainder, no single domain. Morality, as something distinct and discussable, is the exhausted heir of dead religions, and it has been kept going on life-support systems and in intensive care, owing to the assiduity of academic philosophers. Cut off the life-support systems and open the windows: then we can discuss literature and personality in some gentlemanly and non-professional style.

The Nietzschean error can be represented in one word: politics. Nietzsche lived alone, metaphorically if not literally, in lodging-houses and abroad, as remote as possible from the banal transactions of politics and from community life in any form. He had nothing permanently useful to say about political institutions and policies and about their part in limiting tyranny and oppression and in averting the destruction of humanity. Furthermore, it is false, as a matter of historical fact, that morality as a unified domain is the heir of religion and that its integrity has been preserved by professors, as Nietzscheans sometimes pretend. Very similar speculations about the derivation of justice as unique among the virtues, and about absolute and relative duties, antedate by several centuries the Christian era, both in the West and in the East; Nietzsche himself of course acknowledged this.

Perhaps speculation about the universal and rational component in the concept of justice has become more urgent because the danger of total destruction in wars of ideology and of religion now seems notably greater. Contrary to the simple-minded historical relativism traceable to Hegel's influence, the problem in moral philosophy of combining consistency in theory with fidelity to known facts about human nature remains much the same; the problems have not greatly changed in the changing social conditions. Past theories and their critics have revealed blind alleys, and we can stand on the shoulders of the moral philosophers of the past and try to come closer both to the facts of human nature and to new social conditions. But one could sit in the same room with Thucydides, Plato, Aristotle, Montaigne, Hobbes, Montesquieu, Adam Smith, Hume, Kant, Burke, Mill, and Tocqueville, and one could read a paper on procedural justice to this gathering. In the discussion that followed it would be clear that everyone present was talking about the same subject, and that it was certainly not a subject sustained only by a university syllabus. The discussion would touch on the perennial topics of the underpinnings and origins of justice, of the universal and conventional elements in justice, and of the relation of private to public morality.

5

Morality and Machiavelli

❦ The great civilisations of the past have not been created and sustained principally by quietly virtuous persons with a delicate sense of justice. On the contrary they have generally been the products, or the by-products, of overweening ambition and of a large appetite for power and glory. Sometimes the appetite for great wealth, fully displayed, and for refinements of luxury has been the motive for the building of cities, churches, and palaces, and for the encouragement and protection of artists. The surviving cities, sacred buildings, and palaces, and the surviving works of art, are the inherited capital from which an income of excitement, pleasure, and instruction has been derived over many centuries, and will continue to be derived. In addition there are the immense legacies received from past civilisations and populations which form the immaterial capital of mankind: systems of law, sacred texts, secular poetry and prose, musical traditions, systems of social manners, applied arts and domestic skills. Some of this vast inheritance, more or less fragmentarily preserved, still has its irreplaceable effects in contemporary styles and yields continuing pleasure whenever it is reconstructed and recalled. If, in some very general historical retrospect, we reflect on the various agencies from which these incalculable benefits flow, it is obviously necessary to make many distinctions between different

periods and different places. But usually historians have attributed some constructive role to warlords, monarchs, princely
bishops, bankers and entrepreneurs, and great landlords in
bringing into existence the conditions necessary for the spiritual
gains. The desire for conquest and for domination has had a part
in establishing empires which in their turn have developed and
fostered memorable civilisations. In the development of civilisations the Medici family in Machiavelli's Florence are very far
from an exceptional case of the connection between the drive for
domination and the flourishing of the imaginative arts in a highly
civilised, if also cruel, city.

Machiavelli's Problem

❡ It is natural to take Italian examples to illustrate the principle
that many of the flowers of high civilisation grow from the moral
mire of conquest, cruelty, and domination. It is natural because
of Machiavelli, who in the Christian era first and most clearly
presented the central problem of the intersection between politics
and morality. It is disturbing to a moralist that the higher spiritual values of civilisation can often be traced back to violence and
aggression as the necessary conditions of their first realisation.
Machiavelli's problem is more simple still: justice is the opposite
of aggression, conquest, domination, violence, and deceit. Yet
all these denials of justice are indispensable means to secure the
survival of any city or state under any foreseeable conditions of
political life. Machiavelli argued that it was irresponsible for a
man to hold a great office of state, and to establish himself as a
leader in his city, and yet be unwilling to use deceit, violence,
and treachery in defence of the state when it became necessary.
In *The Prince* and in *The Discourses on Livy* he argued that there
would unavoidably arise emergencies in the life span of any state
or city in which extreme measures of cruelty and of violence
would be required in defence of the security of the state. A man
who was not at all times fully prepared for such measures would
not in fact remain in power for long, and he would put his country at risk while he remained in power.

From the Roman Empire until Machiavelli's lifetime it had remained a constant in political calculation that the people require their rulers to be, before all things, strong and resolute, and, when necessary, ruthless and violent. The people, according to Machiavelli, despise weakness and admire the power and the will to crush all opposition without hesitation. They are even ready to be dominated and bullied, provided that they can feel safe and protected against civil strife at home and against enemies abroad. They are reassured rather than morally shocked when their ruler or rulers are cruel, cunning, and effective in destroying those who dare to challenge their power. If Machiavelli returned to study modern democracies, he would be reassured to find that the great majority of voters in every democracy consistently support their government when it is successfully aggressive in the face of foreign powers.

In his two major works, *The Prince* and *The Discourses,* Machiavelli gives an unsurpassed account of the salient conditions of political action. I do not believe that the changes that have occurred in the last three hundred years have made his account out of date, at least from the standpoint of moral philosophy. In many parts of the world modern communications have made the secrets of government less secret than they used to be, and this makes tyranny more open to challenge. But the central dilemmas of power remain: deceit and guile, unjust violence and sudden aggression, ingratitude in relations with allies and friends, are still everyday weapons of government in most parts of the world—unashamedly in some, less flagrantly elsewhere. Machiavelli is particularly vivid in his descriptions of unpredictable reversals of fortune which demand powers of bold improvisation and of sudden and decisive changes of plan. A successful political leader is always rather loose in his thinking, flexible, not bound by principles or by theories, not bound even by his own intentions. He is more like a burglar who is ready to change direction when he runs up against an obstacle in the dark.

Machiavelli dwells with passionate intensity on the conflict between the commitments and obligations of a responsible political leader and the commitments and obligations of the prevailing

Christian morality of his time. He rightly insisted that the two moralities were totally incompatible. Two radically opposed conceptions of the human good are involved, with two sets of commitments and supporting obligations, which no one could reconcile or combine in his conduct. The Christian conception of the good entails that behaviour as God's servant on earth is a preparation for eternal life and salvation hereafter, and that success and failure, virtue and vice, in a lifetime on earth are to be judged within this supernatural perspective. The Last Judgment will reverse the worldly verdict of fame and success. Machiavelli, adviser to the prince, conceives of the good for man as *virtù,* prowess, and virtuosity, which bring glory in the visible achievements of war and of diplomacy, and which bring a permanent place in the history of one's city or state. The great heroes of pagan antiquity, and particularly the heroes of the Roman Republic, are the lasting models of human virtue, calling on ages of comparative decadence for the revival of civic ambition, and for a sense that it is still possible to capture for oneself a glorious role in history, a truly illustrious life.

One side in the Machiavellian conflict is under-represented in this book: the Christian morality which requires self-abnegation and humility in this life with a view to eternal salvation and to glory hereafter. This conception of the good makes holiness the primary moral virtue, and the monastic way of life becomes more noble and more admirable than the way of life of a political leader. Perhaps Machiavelli's conflict between two conceptions of the good becomes even sharper if the hope of supernatural salvation is replaced by the bleak negations of procedural justice, which come into conflict with the drive for power and glory and for great achievements on the stage of history. Can the duties and obligations of fairness and justice, of a minimum level of decency in dealing with persons who have incompatible conceptions of the good, survive the challenges of political expediency?

Machiavelli is surely correct to insist on the reality of the challenges of expediency, and on their unforgiving nature. A political leader who allows a commitment to fair dealing and to substantial justice in all circumstances to override his determination to retain power, and to protect the interests of his country, will surely become ineffective and impotent; and such a person would generally have done better never to have sought or accepted public responsibilities. The first indictment in Machiavelli's polemic is directed against divided purposes and against moral confusion. The virtues that bring great political achievements and civic glory have their cost in the loss of integrity and in the loss of the virtues and the satisfactions of friendship and of fair dealing. The virtues that are essential to an admirable private life, such as loyal friendships and a sense of personal honour and of integrity, have their cost in political powerlessness. A weak and philosophically confused person cannot understand that every kind of human excellence comes from a strong concentration of energies and that it always has its consequent cost. Such a person dissipates his energies and falls short of any form of human excellence. All virtue, like all genuine learning, results from a specialisation of human powers.

Machiavelli himself is an advocate of one specific conception of the good, a conception that is far more widespread and influential than is generally acknowledged in books on moral philosophy. The human good in this conception consists in glorious worldly achievements which will be recognised in history: everyone ought to aspire to some form of memorable greatness, as far as he or she can. The most evident form of greatness is supreme political power, the power of a successful statesman. Under post-Renaissance conditions in Europe glory could also come from great possessions, which lead to munificence and to splendours that will remain visible for centuries.

Glory is not a concept that has played much part in recent moral philosophy, but it has had a place in many past conceptions of the good. Parents often wish their children to have visible worldly success, and prominent positions in their society, rather than commonplace happiness. They can often be seen to take pride in their children's renown and to have developed their children's gifts with a view to glory of some particular kind. To have glory entails being conspicuously admired and having displayed some great virtue, and to enjoy glory in one's lifetime is one possible route to happiness. Glory need not take the harsh Machiavellian forms of political and military victory. When great writers—Hume, Boswell, Gibbon—sought literary fame as a supreme good, they were seeking the glory of achievement, just as the Olympic athlete does. Glory can be a form of transcendence, as Vauvenargues argued and Stendhal understood, an escape into happiness from the humdrum disappointments of everyday living and its dull satisfactions—in this respect comparable with romantic love. Practitioners of all the performing arts aim at the sudden glory of a perfect performance, the radiance of inspiration when the limits set on their skills seem to drop away. Not only in the well-attested case of literature, but in all the arts, the glory of achievement, of working out what must be done in this particular work, is a large part of the conception of the human good that most artists in all ages naturally have had.

In Machiavelli's intensely worldly conception of the good nothing in human experience can be as desirable and satisfying as success in the "great game" of politics—more specifically, the building up of the strength of a city or nation which will itself play a part in the grand history of great cities and great nations. This conception of the good entails that the essential human virtues are those dispositions and powers which are indispensable in a statesman and in a man of action: courage, decisiveness, clearheadedness, energy, the capacity to inspire respect and also fear, single-mindedness in the pursuit of power. Gentleness, and the disposition to foster friendships, and the habit of always being just and fair, are conspicuous among the classical virtues which have to be sacrificed as a cost of the pursuit of historical greatness. A Machiavellian accepts the cost. Machiavelli's worldliness rested on a profound respect for history as the only true warrant and reward of virtue, and as the only attainable transcendence of death. In the Christian era the aspiration to greatness in the light of secular history had been undermined, and Machiavelli proposed that the aspiration should be revived through the study of history itself. For the whole Christian era, at least up till 1789, history as a study, and humanistic studies generally, were animated by the twin problems of why the Roman Empire collapsed and how modern Europe may finally emerge from its decadence and recapture the greatness of the ancient pagan cities. This at least was the secular spirit wherever it could survive outside the Church, and sometimes within it, as with Richelieu.

The decadence of modern nations, that is, their disunity and their loss of civic ambitions and of republican virtues, is attributable, according to Machiavelli, to the ethics of renunciation, the ethics of innocence and of self-abnegation, which had not been known in the ancient world. The morality of innocence is the morality of a people who are resigned to being impotent. Those populations within which this conception of the good prevails will disappear from history without trace, leaving few models or monuments as their inheritance. They have looked for their reward and their glory in heaven, and, whether or not they find them there, they will be fittingly forgotten here.

One part of Machiavelli's problem can be separated from Machiavelli's ethics: the ethics of glory in action and of greatness in history. The evident incompatibility between strict attention to justice and fairness on the one side and effectiveness in the exercise of political power raises a deep problem, even when effectiveness in politics is not taken as an overriding end. I have tried to make Machiavelli's morality plausible and interesting, because I believe this morality always has had, and still has, more influence in people's thought than is generally acknowledged. Whenever a person, in France or in England or in Japan or in China, finds comfort for personal disappointments in the history and predominance of her people, the power of their institutions, their language, their arts, their literature, she is thinking of history as redeeming the transitoriness of the present and as redeeming the comparatively trivial span of an individual's life. She is thinking also of participating in a glory which will survive and be remembered. When imperial power diminishes and disappears, and when other forms of national predominance disappear with it, there is a sense of loss among the population, almost as if it were a personal or family loss.

Machiavelli's problem cannot be plausibly evaded or blurred by stressing the cruelties and injustices peculiar to Renaissance princes in Italy; examples from our century can easily support the argument. If it is true that injustice, the use of force and violence, deceit and treachery are occasional necessities in the effective exercise of political power, is it not impossible that a just and good person can ever exercise political power or enter into governments which will use such methods? Have I not argued that minimum, procedural justice is an absolute duty independent of all conceptions of the good, and, further, that the very opposite of the virtue of justice and fairness, of the minimum of moral decency in public affairs, is the disposition to dominate, the refusal to negotiate?

The problem has to be approached from the standpoint of persons who have decisions to make about their future conduct. Because it is a moral problem, it is best interpreted as a practical problem, that is, as a problem confronting someone who is wondering what he ought to do. There is no reason why moral philosophers should assume the roles of Rhadamanthus or Saint Peter, and ask themselves how they are to deliver verdicts in some last judgment on the lives of morally innocent and just persons, innocent of political action, as contrasted with the lives of some politically constructive persons, who have treated people unfairly and unjustly when political expediency demanded it. We will perplex ourselves unnecessarily if we assume that all human beings have willy-nilly been entered as competitors in a single moral steeplechase, and that we need criteria for allotting them points on their performance.

Towards a Reply

❦ Before trying to solve Machiavelli's problem of political innocence and political experience, it would be well for me to set out again the positions for which I have so far argued:

1. There are many different conceptions of the good which are defensible by reference to reasonable arguments, drawing on both personal experience and historical evidence.

2. Some conceptions of the good, including well-known and ancient conceptions, are indefensible, in the sense that, when challenged, their defenders base their beliefs on errors, whether of fact or of theory or of logic, and no better reasons have been found for accepting them.

3. Some conceptions of the good are absolutely evil, because they directly encourage unlimited domination and they eliminate respect for minimum procedural justice.

4. The minimum concept of justice is trans-historical, being rooted in the indispensable institutions of civil society, within which people deliberate together, argue over practical issues, adjudicate between cases. There are also changing conceptions of substantial justice derived from changing conceptions of the good.

5. The concept of justice gets its sense from a minimum fairness in established procedures of settling conflicts, national and international, by argument and negotiation and by quasi-legal reasoning.

6. A minimum of decent fairness, both in personal relations and in public affairs, is a value independent of any conception of the good. It is rooted in the fact that human beings have to some degree the habit of balancing contrary arguments and of drawing conclusions from them. Minimum justice is the elaborate application of this habit to interpersonal relations, entailing fair rules of procedure.

With these propositions as background Machiavelli's problem is not altogether intractable. First, almost all men and women are naturally guided towards political innocence or towards political experience by their own temperaments and talents, and by their circumstances and opportunities. Whether they should become involved in the pursuit of political power is not usually a question that presents itself in the abstract. A person's particular capacities and interests, his particular situation and opportunities, determine, or at least constrain, the outcome. Most people in all periods have no access to real political power, most lack any interest in real political power, and only a minority of persons in any period ever confront Machiavelli's problem in the concrete circumstances of their own lives. But this fact does not make the problem unimportant from the moral point, if only because everyone's way of life at all times depends for its survival on the virtues and achievements of politicians. The safety of the morally innocent, and their freedom to lead their own lives, depend upon the rulers' clear-headedness in the use of power. If their rulers are too weak, too scrupulous, too inexperienced, or too pure, their innocent pursuits of the good, however conceived, will sooner or later be disrupted.

What can reasonably be demanded of those who incur the responsibility of political power? The first demand is that they should recognise the weight of their peculiar responsibility in disposing of the lives of others. The second is that they should be clear-headed, and not divided in mind, about their obligations to protect the reasonable interests of their innocent fellow citizens; this is the Machiavellian thesis. The third demand is that they should at all times be prepared for the occurrence of an uncontrolled conflict of duties in situations which seem to exclude the possibility of a decent outcome, and in which all lines of action seem dishonourable or blameworthy. This is the point at which the contrast between innocence and experience becomes indispensable in ethics. The idea of experience is the idea of guilty knowledge, of the expectation of unavoidable squalor and imperfection, of necessary disappointments and mixed results, of half success and half failure. A person of experience has come to expect that his usual choice will be of the lesser of two or more evils. In the normal circumstances of private and working life, outside high politics, a person can usually pursue chosen ends with some confidence of anticipating the situations that will be encountered along the way. Not so in politics, as every experienced leader from Thucydides onwards has remarked. The excitement of political experience, which some find irresistible and some repellent, consists in the struggle with fortune, in which power may be lost or won in the chosen response to a sudden turn of events. It is difficult to exaggerate the width of the gap between the virtues of a political commentator and theorist on one side and the virtues of someone actually exercising power as a ruler and leader on the other side. Even a very good historian is unable to communicate vividly enough the rush of uncertainties amid which decisions of great consequence are typically made.

By what method should the conflict between justice and political expediency be resolved in any particular case? What is the scale on which in any particular case the balance should be struck? The metaphor of striking a balance, which naturally suggests itself, already indicates what the method is. If a minority is victimised and forfeits some of its rights, the injustice would in some cases be justifiable, if the risk to national security is very great and if the whole population would probably suffer in a national disaster, and if the injury done to the minority is not correspondingly great. In this type of situation, which is not uncommon, the government has to strike a balance between evils. The adversary arguments that it must weigh are partly consequentialist arguments that compare probable outcomes with magnitudes of injustice; partly they involve rights of a fundamental kind and obligations incurred earlier. The government's decision is a just and fair one only if it satisfies the minimum conditions of procedural justice: that the contrary claims are recognised and assessed by reference to their supporting arguments, and that the decision is not made by default. This is a necessary, but not a sufficient, condition of arriving at a just balance. Substantial conceptions of justice, derived from conceptions of the good, must also be involved in assessing the priorities and in counting the losses and gains of the alternatives.

There will always be occasional situations in which the government's action was in the circumstances probably the right action, all things considered and on balance, but it was an action that leaves a sense of horror, and even disgust, behind it. So far

Machiavelli was right. But he exaggerates the role of *raison d'état* in political prudence and morality, leaving the impression that it ought always, or almost always, to prevail over considerations of fairness and justice to individuals and groups. Machiavelli over-simplified his own problem in those passages in which he seems to maintain that a ruler must take the security of the state as an overriding consideration in all conceivable circumstances, even if this involves him in trampling on the common decencies of min-imum justice in acts of state terrorism that are typical of tyran-nies. There is no consideration of any kind that overrides all other considerations in all conceivable circumstances.

The exercise of reason in public affairs is distinguished from its normal use in private life by its negativity; it seems unavoid-able that, in the exercise of political power, one should very often, perhaps usually, be choosing between two evils, and trying to prevent the greater misery and the worse injustice. A government is required to improvise in the emergencies which are bound to occur in the unceasing struggle for power between states and between parties and social groups within states. An innocent interlude is not to be expected by anyone who possesses real political power.

Innocence and Experience Illustrated

❡ The contrast between innocence and experience is so deep and so pervasive, from the moral point of view, that it probably needs some concrete illustration; otherwise it remains an abstrac-tion. Consider an early Quaker meeting house with freshly whitewashed walls, rather worn and polished benches and hand-rails, and no pictures or representations of any kind, no altar, no decoration, no centre to the room and no raised dais, no desig-nated spaces for rituals and sacraments. As soon as you open the heavy oak door and step inside, you are aware of stillness, purity of outline, and cleanness, of the absence of distractions and en-cumbrances, of the invitation to quiet reflection. The world and its business have been shut out for the sake of absolute quietness and of a consequent turning inwards. One can easily in such surroundings imagine the steady gaze, the healthy colour and the stiff, starched linen and plain broadcloth of the early Quakers at their meetings, free from the distractions of ritual and from any thought of the historical compromises involved in the publicly rehearsed creeds. History and memory are not celebrated in the Quaker meeting house, as they are in all the churches in Rome. The grave individual conscience, alone with its own spontaneous and troubled thoughts and its own hesitations, is here the centre of religious ethics. Each soul must strain towards an entirely authentic belief, an entirely true witness, purged of all pretence and all inherited conventions and authorities. The singleness of each person is essential, though not the separateness. The Quaker community has met in this place for centuries; but the community was a pool constantly re-filled from pure and single springs.

It is easy to see why the men and women who met here would be inclined to turn away from moral complexities and from ambiguous situations, and why they would become pacifists and conscientious objectors. Their conception of the good was a vision of simplicity, whiteness, straightness, uprightness, cleanness, of sweeping away anything contaminated or corrupted or squalid. Why should one meditate on one's life as if in a moral half-light and behind stained glass, however beautifully elaborated, when one could allow the rays of sunlight to shine through clear windows on to clean walls? Nothing needs to be concealed, and there is no need for whispering in confessionals in dark corners. It is possible for each man or woman to start again with a simplified picture of the world, and not to admit to this purified world any of the gaudy furniture of moral compromise inherited from the history of the churches. The Quaker conception of the good life is necessarily an innocent life, uncontaminated by violence, and by deceit and luxury, and by the complex and unclean calculations which support violence and deceit and luxury. The early Quakers, as I have imagined them, stand at the opposite end of the scale of worldliness from Machiavelli, allowing no place in their conception of moral responsibility for military conquest and well-timed chicanery.

The opposed conception of the good, associated with experience, can be illustrated by the chancelleries and palaces of the great European capitals, with their gilded and glittering staterooms designed in imitation of Versailles; or, perhaps even better, by the corridors, ceremonial rooms, and chapels of the Vatican, a storehouse of works of art and monuments from the Church's often turbulent history. In the Vatican the weight and splendour of the institution, and the continuity of its story, seem to overwhelm the single individuals who have played, and are playing, a glorious part within the institution. The Church has lived through innumerable wars, periods of exile, negotiations, unwanted compromises, embarrassing alliances, distressing manoeuvres, and secret betrayals. Those who come to power within the Church will be expected always to understand its present predicaments in the light of its history. They will not be deceived by any too straightforward and simple statement of the Church's purposes, purposes that are always being subtly modified to meet changing circumstances. Certainly they are not expected to see in the Church's problems an occasion for vindicating some ideal of personal integrity, or for observing the principles of humility and innocence which have plausibly been associated with primitive Christianity and with the Gospels. As members of the government of the Church, the cardinals and bishops have a primary duty to contribute to the welfare and the power of the Church and to the long-term fulfilment of its sacred mission. Their conception of the good certainly includes their relation to God as individual persons; but it also includes success in promoting the interests of the Church and in defending the Church against its enemies. This is a political activity and famously requires something of "the cunning of the serpent", the ingenuity of worldly wisdom, which Aristotle claimed that both rogues and statesmen need.

In chancelleries and palaces, and in the corridors of secular power, ideals of personal integrity and of moral innocence are kept in abeyance. An overriding loyalty is owed, according to one conception of the good, to an institution of which one is part or to a political cause which one believes to be substantially just. This loyalty provides duties which in many circumstances override the duties of personal integrity, honesty, friendship, and gentleness. Persons having this conception of the good, who have always existed, are not subverters of all morality. They have a distinct and defensible notion of moral responsibility. Such a responsible politician is always ready to negotiate, and to make a deal, in the best interests, as he conceives them, of the institution or political entity for which he holds himself responsible. He assumes that there is a necessary limit to the morally inspired wars of all against all. The limit is set by shared habits of negotiation and of bargaining, which entail the exchange of concessions judged in the particular circumstances to be a fair exchange.

An irresponsible Machiavellian, or a morbid realpolitiker, can persuade himself that all political negotiations, when fully analysed, can be seen to have outcomes that are wholly determined by the power relationships among the parties involved, and that the supporting arguments are epiphenomenal, mere decoration, without effect and uncorrelated with the conclusion. This is the equivalent of scepticism about practical reason in its private and individual employment as deliberation, when a person gives herself reasons for her actions. The sceptic says that such reasons are always rationalisations, that is, they are without effect, dynamically inert, mere decoration, designed to make the agent respectable in her own eyes and in the eyes of others. The actions so disguised are always best explained by the relative strength of the desires of the agent at the time of action.

Both in its political and in its private form this scepticism about practical reason is implausible for many reasons, and particularly because the notion of desire involved is absurdly oversimplified in the individual case. In the public case the sceptic, seduced by a mechanical model, overlooks the active interest that men and women observably take both in the process and in the procedures of negotiation. Human beings are by nature not only image-making and drug-taking animals, seeking transcendence by making pictures and through the chemistry of plants; they are also argumentative and litigious animals, observably taking delight in the rituals and procedures of argument, advocacy, and negotiation. The various, and sometimes perverse, practices of law come naturally to them, no less than the various and perverse practices of sexuality. Rhetoric has always engaged men's imaginations, and the desire to win an argument can be as intense as the desire to win a race. Most conspicuously in high politics, delight in the exercise of political skills in negotiation, and in the calculation of probable outcomes, often outweighs, or at least greatly complicates, an interest in the ultimate ends to be achieved. It is easy to underestimate the acute professional pleasure that politicians of sharply hostile purposes may take in their negotiations with each other and in the processes of manoeuvre and counter-manoeuvre. They recognise and respect in each other a passion and a pleasure, sometimes almost an addiction, which they do not share with the unpolitical mass of mankind. In this respect they resemble artists who, in spite of widely divergent purposes in their art, may recognize and respect in each other the concentration of technical skill in execution which an amateur would not notice and would not understand. In both cases the professionals feel at ease with their own kind. Richelieu, William III of England, Cavour, Franklin D. Roosevelt, Lloyd George were all men who pursued serious and constructive political purposes; but they also possessed a passion for political intrigue, and for all the complexities of political calculation. Alongside the pursuit of power through violence and the threat of violence, there are contrary impulses, equally natural, that support the virtue of procedural justice, as this is interpreted at a particular place and time. Procedural justice is supported by the impulses and the temperament which create lawyers and orators, who instinctively see power as persuasion rather than as conquest, and who cultivate and enjoy the skills of bargaining and of debate.

To summarise: Machiavelli's problem, the conflict between personal honour and public responsibility, has only a complicated answer, at least on a philosophical level. First must come a concession to Machiavelli: in general, it is true that moral innocence and purity are incompatible with the effective exercise of political power on any considerable scale, and that two conceptions of virtue and of responsible action, attached to two very different ways of life, have to be recognised; and they have to be recognised as a duality that persists through all periods of history. The opposition between private and public virtue is a philosophical concern just because it does not arise from particular historical circumstances. Rather it introduces an unchanging ambiguity into the notion of virtue. Plato laboured in the *Republic* to close the gap between private and public virtue with his analogy between justice in the soul and justice in the state, but unconvincingly. The virtues of innocence, which are not necessarily the "monkish virtues", realise conceptions of the good which can inspire strong emotions and great admiration: absolute integrity, gentleness, disposition to sympathy, a fastidious sense of honour, generosity, a disposition to gratitude. The virtues of experience can equally inspire strong emotions and great admiration: tenacity and resolution, courage in the face of risk, intelligence, largeness of design and purpose, exceptional energy, habits of leadership.

A philosopher in his study is in no position to lay down rules for justified murders and reasonable treachery. Nor can one determine *a priori* what degree of achievement outweighs what degrees of inhumanity in the means employed. Once again the philosophical point to be recorded is that there is no completeness and no perfection to be found in morality.

History Again

❡ It is difficult to exaggerate the part that the idea of history has played in many conceptions of the good. In Machiavelli's *The Prince* and in *The Discourses on Livy* history becomes the stage upon which the political hero displays his virtue in always memorable action, as if his campaigns are works of art to be preserved in the annals of a heroic past. The inherited glory of the people to which one belongs is both an incentive to the virtue of an individual and an indispensable condition of virtue, according to Machiavelli. Similarly in the speech attributed to Pericles in Thucydides' *History of the Peloponnesian War;* the Athenians as individuals are encouraged to take pride in the glorious monuments of their city, and to develop their distinct individualities as only Athenians can. As a dangerous war begins, they are expected to rise to the historic occasion and to make their contribution to the annals of their city. Thucydides and Machiavelli are obviously to be counted among the classic authors of historical rhetoric. During the nineteenth century, the great age of modern historical studies, this rhetoric was debased in countless nationalistic speeches and was reduced to banality in the popular histories of nation-states. Later generations in Europe have in consequence tired of these tales of past glories. Machiavelli's theory of history was like a neo-classical building, a lively imitation of ancient models, and the nationalist rhetoric of the last two centuries can be compared with the architecture of a modern bank, which has a neo-classical facade that has lost the classical spirit.

In spite of this fading of conceptions of the good associated with historical glory, morality is generally associated in the Western world with some theory of history, explicit or unexpressed. Most of the moral systems that emerged from the thought of the Enlightenment tell a story of the emancipation of the human mind as a progress in history, as in Condorcet, or as later in Hegel and Marx. The teaching of the historical religions and of these later philosophies has seeped into the common consciousness in the West. The consequences are evident whenever moral issues in important areas of ordinary life are debated: discussions of sexual morality, of equal rights for women, of the morality of property and ownership, of crime and punishment. Consider first contemporary discussions of sexual morality. Often one hears the point: "One cannot put the clock back. What was morally acceptable in the past cannot be morally acceptable now with modern technology and with modern communications: our morality should change in parallel with social change." This pull towards historical relativism has become part of popular culture, and popular culture must enter into prevailing moral ideas. Prevailing moral ideas are the raw data and starting-point for the speculations of moral philosophers, who will try to clarify them and sometimes, while clarifying, to amend them. The place for drastic amendment, I believe, is precisely at the conception of history which has formed this popular moral relativism.

Hegelianism, positivism, Marxism, constructed in the shadow of Christianity with a view to its replacement, purported to give an account of the development of mankind as a whole, an account of the destiny of the species: this included an alienation or fall, followed by a political and social redemption, leading to a final salvation of humanity. From the standpoint of a naturalistic philosophy, looking only at the so far known facts of human history, the gross implausibility of these accounts comes from the false speciation and the false humanism. "Humanity" is either the name of a distinct animal species, with impressively distinct powers of mind and with an uncertain future, or it is the name of a class of being constituted as distinct by the intention of its Creator; and of course the name may sometimes be used with both meanings in mind. If the supernatural claims about the Creator's intentions are dismissed, there remains no sufficient empirical reason to believe that there is such a thing as the historical development of mankind as a whole, unless the natural history of the evolution of the species is intended. What we see in history is the ebb and flow of different populations at different stages of social development, interacting with each other and exhibiting no common pattern of development. Using older historical categories, we can reasonably speak of the various populations flourishing and becoming powerful at some stage and then falling into decadence and becoming comparatively weak; and historians can reasonably look for some general causes of these rises and falls. Even if some such general causes can be found, they will not by themselves point to a destiny, and to an order of development, for mankind as a whole.

Ways of life evidently come to be and pass away, together with the conceptions of the good that animate them. The bewildering ebb and flow of separate histories in separate places composes one half of what we know about human nature: the other half comes from the natural sciences. The philosophical difficulty is to preserve the same unsullied respect for fact in face of the historical evidence which we are constrained to keep in biology. If we do not respect the facts in biology, and if we indulge ourselves with tidy and comforting general theories, we encounter recalcitrant experiences. We have to stop and to admit ignorance; we do not purchase coherence at the cost of truth. In studying the evidence about ways of life which have existed in the past, a historian's explanatory hypotheses are not similarly exposed to direct falsification. There is for this reason a temptation to impose some pattern of development in describing past ways of life, and to pick out the facts which fit into the pattern. Any historical explanation of past ways of life is threatened with this circularity.

Everyone has an emotional interest in discerning coherent patterns of development in his or her own life. The notions of individual responsibility and of individual character demand that a coherent pattern of development should be discernible. This notion of responsibility, and even the idea of a distinctive character and set of dispositions, can sometimes plausibly be transferred to a population living and acting together, as in a tribe or in an ancient city or in a nation-state. A population may contain a majority who feel that the nation made itself responsible for its present miseries by its misguided ambitions in the past. Irrationality begins when this sense of responsibility, and the sense of the past that goes with it, are transferred to humanity as a whole. Humanity is not yet a population which lives and works together, and humanity does not carry a weight of responsibility. Only those who claim insight into the Creator's intentions can reasonably claim that it does.

If we can recover from the dream of teleological philosophies of history, and if we are ready to acknowledge the untidy variety of moralities revealed by anthropologists and historians, morality can be brought back to its real sources: first, to the memories, imaginations, and emotions of individuals forming conceptions of a good way of life within a particular culture and language, and, second, to universal practical reasoning and adversary argument, by which persons try to resolve both their inner and their interpersonal conflicts, including conflicting conceptions of the good. It is not only within a single society but also within a single mind that competing conceptions of the good are weighed, incompatible virtues sought, conflicting duties recognised. It is normal for souls to be in conflict, pulled by impulse towards different ways of life, just as it is normal for there to be conflicts of ideals and interests within every society. Absence of conflict, single-mindedness, whether within the soul or within the state, is a possible part of a possible conception of the good, but certainly not a necessary one.

Stability and the absence of conflict in the mind, coherence and harmony among different interests, have been part of the conception of the good in philosophers as different in other respects as Plato and Spinoza. Theirs is the moral ideal of rationalists, who look to the aristocratic dominance of reason to impose stability in the soul, in parallel with the dominance of an intellectual elite who will impose stability in society through a proper subordination of an unenlightened lower class. This traditional rationalism has no place for negotiation, in the soul and in the state, partly because such compromises will always be unstable. They will be temporary settlements and precarious balances, both in the soul and in the state, without the police forces of the will, as in Plato's *Republic,* to repress unruly interests at the command of pure reason. The work of practical reason in arbitrating between competing interests is never finished, never final and secure. Surveying any tract of history, and looking into our own minds, we see the ebb and flow of contrary passions and interests needing to be reconciled; in the mind by that form of inner adjudication which is called reflection, and in the state by the literal and visible adjudications of parliaments and law courts.

The watery metaphors, such as "ebb and flow", seem unavoidable in this context: Montaigne wrote of the undulating notions of the mind and Spinoza of the fluctuation of the passions. The implicit purpose of these Heraclitean metaphors is to dissolve the mechanical and deterministic models that we apply both to the forces and tendencies that we think we discern in the mind, and to the forces and tendencies that we think we discern in history. A wave is apparently a thing which does not behave in the deterministic style of a particle, and which does not have the distinctly bounded parts that machines have. The desires and interests that we identify in our minds at any one time merge with and interpenetrate each other in a watery way, and there is some distortion in our habit of representing them as distinct and labelled drives and levers. Similarly, the distinct forces at work within a state, the distinct social groups, even the distinct cultures in history, are convenient abstractions only, which are not to be taken too seriously as elements in explanation. Social groups and historical cultures merge and interpenetrate and have dubious boundaries, just as distinguishable ways of life merge and interpenetrate in a watery manner. The ultimate concrete reality, from the moral point of view, is to be found in the behaviour, and in the communicable thoughts and feelings, of individual persons.

I have mentioned Plato's analogy between justice in the soul and justice in the state partly in order to stress the fact that in describing the operations of the mind we are driven to use transferred terms and metaphors, taken from the public realm of objects and of commonly observed operations. Many of these transferred terms in their literal employment refer to government and to social relations, and the picture of faculties of the mind conveyed is a reflection of past social philosophies. To look for the foundations of morality in these metaphors is to look in soft and shifting ground.

The second reason for continuing to stress Plato's analogy between governance of the soul and governance of the state is to explain how our sense of justice in practical reasoning arises. Here we are dealing not with metaphors, but rather with a set of human practices which are observable in every part of the world and throughout history: the practices of negotiation when there are adversary claims. These practices and the institutions associated with them engender the canons of just and fair practical reasoning, the norms of procedural justice and fairness.

Between the public and the private adjudications, in the inner forum of the mind, there is one notable difference: public deliberations always have clearly marked parts and stages, while private deliberations, generally speaking, do not. On the other hand it is inconceivable that there should be public adjudications, and weighings of alternatives in council chambers, without corresponding processes and procedures in the minds of the councillors; the public and private procedures are inextricably tied together. The universal requirement of procedural justice is present to the mind, not in virtue of some allegedly self-evident proposition, as in the theory of natural law, but in virtue of practices without which any form of shared human life is unimaginable.

Justice and the Dispossessed

❦ In successive periods of history the demands of the dispossessed for recognition and for redress have often been expressed as appeals for substantial justice. But the demands of the dispossessed have also often been expressed, particularly in the last two centuries, as demands for greater freedom or for greater equality. This has been the Jacobin tradition, set in motion by Rousseau and passing to Robespierre, the tradition of revolution that came to life again in the Paris Commune of 1870. Socialist parties in Europe have later drawn on the Jacobin concept of equality when prescribing the moral goal of a socialist transformation of society. They have sometimes also invoked the Jacobin conception of freedom, which entails that every citizen feels that he or she is an equal member of a self-governing community which pursues the common good. Both the ideal of social equality, and the ideal of the Rousseauesque community of free citizens, are elements in an imaginative conception of the good. There is no compelling reason to be found in the universal practices of mankind to claim that citizenship in a genuine community is always to be preferred, and is always intrinsically better, than citizenship in some looser and larger and more atomistic society. Rousseau, and many socialists after him, have legitimately and successfully evoked the emotions that are associated with a communitarian way of life. As moralists they have argued for the superiority of this way of life, and their cause is certain to be divisive and to have enemies.

If socialists argued their case by appeals to substantial justice, rather than in terms of equality and freedom, their cause would still be divisive and have enemies, because a substantial conception of distributive justice is being invoked; therefore some conception of the good is also being invoked. Is it unjust and unfair that so much wealth should accrue to financiers, landowners, entrepreneurs, and managers and so little should be earned by labourers engaged in arduous and tedious work? Is the contrast in a single place between great wealth and abject poverty less of an evil than the methods which would be necessary to eliminate it? Conservatives, liberals, and socialists will derive different answers to these two questions from their different conceptions of the human good, and therefore of what is just and right. But all three groups, including the socialists, will think more clearly about the issues of poverty, property, and property rights, if they see their disagreements as disagreements about substantial justice. The concept of justice provides a common framework within which the points of divergence can be clearly marked, and traced to their sources in different psychological, historical, metaphysical, and religious beliefs, beliefs which support different conceptions of the good.

If the conflict over conceptions of justice supplies the framework within which the political conflict is fought out, there will be some congruity between the means used to impose any temporary settlement that emerges and the settlement itself. There will not be that incongruity between means and ends which was evident in Robespierre's Jacobinism and which descended to Lenin's "democratic centralism" and thereafter to the domination of the Communist Party in communist countries.

Socialist parties in European democracies have been misguided when they ground their moral appeals in the ideal of equality rather than of justice, following the thought and rhetoric of the French revolutionary tradition. The implicit moral appeal of *Das Kapital* is to the in-built unfairness of the distribution of property under capitalism, which ensures, according to Marx, that the labourer can never receive the just rewards of his labour, which will be skimmed off as surplus value and distributed to the owners and controllers of the means of production. That is the core of the moral argument, without its pseudo-scientific clothing. This argument links the nineteenth-century factory worker and agricultural labourer as victims of injustice to the dispossessed of previous ages: to slaves in the ancient world and in the American South and elsewhere; to conquered populations everywhere, untouchables, ethnic minorities without citizen's rights; to landless peasants, and to all those who have nothing themselves and who depend on the will of others for their survival and for the survival of their children. Such persons have no alternatives: they must organise themselves as strongly as they can in order to present an effective demand for justice, which entails that their substantial claims should become a cause of conflict leading sooner or later to serious negotiation. If they achieve no access to fair considerations of their claims, and if they have a reasonable chance of success through violence, they will fight for justice, as they perceive it, until their substantial claims are fairly considered. This has always been the way, the justifiable way, of the dispossessed who have come to feel strongly enough the injustice of which they are the victims and who have been denied the minimum decencies of procedural justice.

There are always open possibilities of improving human life in indefinitely many ways, and among the possibilities is the elimination of gross poverty and of at least some of the risks of war. But practical possibilities exist as such only as long as they are vividly imagined and actively explored. They disappear as practical possibilities when we are deceived by old arguments which represent customary practices as the only natural ones, with the implication that there are no other possible worlds—which would be as natural as the actual one, if we combined to create them.

A Reply to Machiavelli

❦ It ought now to be possible to respond to Machiavelli's challenge. The old opposition between innocence and experience does represent, at a very general level, contrary moral ideals which will not lose their competing attractions, even if their opposition will not always be as strongly reinforced by religion as it was in the past. Metaphors of dirt ("les mains sales") and of purity and whiteness will probably always remain intelligible. G. K. Chesterton remarked that a person's goodness can be something directly encountered and felt like a pain or a smell. This kind of goodness implies a purity of character, a transparency of motive and cleanness of intention, a sense of honour and of integrity, which cannot persist through the moral compromises which hold a party and a government together, and through the occasional cruelties and exploitations involved in statecraft. The answer to Machiavelli must be, first, that there is a recognisable basic level of common decency, which I have tried to analyse with the notion of minimum procedural justice, and that evil, in the form of the drive to domination, consists in the uncompensated violation of this basic justice; and, second, that in weighing in politics conflicting moral claims and competing conceptions of the good, this minimum justice plays the role of the scales, while considerations derived from different conceptions of the good can be seen as the weights that have to be assessed.

To take an example: Caught between his responsibility to protect the standard of living of those he represents on one side, and on the other side a *prima facie* duty to see that a threatened minority is not unjustly treated, a politician weighs two moral claims on him. His own conception of the good, and the substantial conception of justice derived from it, will tip the balance

one way or the other. The basic decency, the universal requirement, is that the politician should establish the nature of the
claims upon him in their own terms before he restates them in
his own terms drawn from his own conception of the good. This
is the judicial function of practical reason in private deliberation,
when there is a conflict of moral claims and not merely a question of means to ends. This function in a decent society is dis-
charged by parliaments, law courts, civil services, with some
recognition and respect for the procedures of just judgment.

There is a complicated story to be told (although not here) of
the relation of minimum and procedural justice to substantial and
variable notions of distributive justice, corrective justice, and social justice: variable because of their derivation from different
conceptions of the good, and because they have their roles in
different ways of life flourishing at different times. The argument
for tyranny, ancient and modern, is always that suspension of the
minimum decencies of procedural justice is to be accepted as necessary to the defence of a particular conception of the human
good: either social equality, or the freedom associated with capitalist enterprise and with the protection of private property.
Then it is discovered that the evil of domination and injustice not
only outweighs, but even partly destroys, the moral gain in social equality and the moral gain of open market freedoms.

It was the great service of John Rawls's book *A Theory of Justice*
to have restored justice to its ancient place as (apart from love
and friendship) almost the whole of virtue in relations between
people, and the first of all virtues in basic social arrangements;
and to have detached justice, and the explication of the sense of
the concept, from the varying conceptions of the good which
different individuals and different cultures may form. In the primary use of the term in his theory, justice was to be attached to
the fundamental institutions of the society, and through them to
the machinery of decision-making in morally substantial questions. So far, so good. But Rawls's political or procedural justice
is, as he defines it, not narrowly procedural enough. Even in his
later accounts of "political liberalism", as he calls it, a well-

ordered democratic society is presupposed, and traditions of intolerance and fanaticism, and denials of moral pluralism, are excluded. Political liberalism includes a definite, although incomplete, conception of the good which prevails principally among free-thinking liberals in politically sophisticated societies. For such persons the liberty of the individual is the first essential element in the good. So-called procedural justice, as Rawls specifies its content, is not acceptable as justice in the judgment of those, for instance, who accept all the traditional authority of the Catholic Church in moral matters; Rawls's just institutions will permit freedom of choice in areas where the devout believe such freedom ought not to be allowed. Again, his version of procedural justice entails an ethics of re-distribution of material advantages, designed to avoid any increase of the differentials between rich and poor. Conservative thinkers who attach high priority to property rights in all their thought about justice cannot accept Rawls's basic institutions as just. Two or more substantial conceptions of just institutions dealing with the distribution of property are usually in conflict in modern societies. In investigating the reasons for these different conceptions, and their implications, one expects to find either that one or both of the rivals are confused in their thinking, or that their different conceptions of just distributions are derived from different conceptions of the human good. The shared basis that makes the negotiation possible is not a set of shared first-order moral beliefs. The shared basis is a set of common practices. Persons of political experience, looking at each other fiercely across the table, are not required to respect each other as entire moral beings: only as reasonable in negotiation, which is just one part of a whole moral being.

At least since Hobbes's *Leviathan,* political philosophers have used the device of the social contract to pick out a set of shared beliefs, or of shared purposes, actual and possible, which can form a consensual meeting-ground for all citizens, whatever the other differences between them are. The hankering after some kind of consensus, which persists in Rawls's theory, is both natural and very strong. It is assumed that there cannot be social stability within nations, and—now perhaps more urgent—peace between nations, unless an implicit consensus is first discovered and then is made explicit and reinforced. The assumption has been that, from the moral point of view, the bedrock of human nature is to be found in self-evident and unavoidable beliefs. But after every attempt the alleged unavoidable beliefs are shown to be either vacuous or, if substantial, dubious, and at least very far from being unavoidable.

We should look in society not for consensus, but for inelimin-able and acceptable conflicts, and for rationally controlled hostil-ities, as the normal condition of mankind; not only normal, but also the best condition of mankind from the moral point of view, both between states and within states. This was Heraclitus's vi-sion: that life, and liveliness, within the soul and within society, consists in perpetual conflicts between rival impulses and ideals, and that justice presides over the hostilities and finds sufficient compromises to prevent madness in the soul, and civil war or war between peoples. Harmony and inner consensus come with death, when human faces no longer express conflicts but are im-mobile, composed, and at rest. To correct Plato's analogy: justice within the soul may be seen as the intelligent recognition and acceptance of conflicting and ambivalent elements in one's own imagination and emotions—not the suppression of conflicts by a dominant intellect for the sake of harmony, but rather their con-tainment through some means of expression peculiar to the in-dividual. In pursuing its changing conceptions of the good, the life of the soul is a series of compromise formations, which are evidently unstable and transient, just as every successive state of society is evidently unstable and transient.

Index

Adjudication, 54–55, 58, 138, 140, 169, 181, 183
Agency, 18
Alienation, 150, 179
Analogy, 64, 65, 97, 105, 106, 123, 182, 189
Aquinas, Thomas, 37
Architectonic classification, 25, 27, 28
Aristotle, 6, 12, 17–35, 40, 41, 46, 51, 53, 56, 67, 71, 72, 105, 110, 115, 133, 135, 139, 157, 174
Association of ideas, 40, 121, 122
Athens, 58, 63
Authoritarians, 142–146, 154
Autonomy, 41, 142

Balance, 27–28
Bergson, Henri, 120, 121, 138
Betrayal, 146, 147
Biological needs, 33, 125
Bradley, F. H., 6
Burke, Edmund, 138, 157

Capitalism, 4, 5, 6, 185
Case law, 62
Categories of being, 120
Causal dependencies, 36

Ceteris paribus clauses, 84, 87, 88, 92
Chance, 101, 115, 119, 128, 132, 133, 147, 185
Chesterton, G. K., 186
Christianity, 7, 64, 70, 76, 77, 104, 108, 116, 136, 150, 157, 162, 164, 166, 167
Church, Catholic, 9, 60, 143, 167, 174, 188
Civic ambition, 164, 167
Civil disobedience, 104
Communism, 5, 9, 10, 136, 150, 184
Community, 43, 60, 61, 70, 73, 135, 138, 154, 157, 172, 183, 184
Compromise, 74, 114, 140, 174, 189
Concordia ordinum, 109
Condorcet, 61, 136, 137, 178
Conquest, 141, 142, 153, 154, 162
Consciousness, 40, 178
Consensus, liberal, 9, 188–189
Consequentialism, 81–82, 130, 171
Conservativism, 5, 6, 77, 103, 143, 154, 155, 184, 188
Convention, 76, 87, 108, 138, 139, 142, 157, 173
Conversion, 103, 133, 153
Correctness, 18

Culture, 8, 46, 60, 119, 131, 141, 179, 182
Customs, 43, 74, 75, 185

Dalai Lama, 120
Deceit, 11, 162, 163, 168, 173
Decency, 8, 13, 33, 68, 106, 164, 168, 169, 170, 172, 185, 186, 187
Definite descriptions, 84–88
Deliberation, 18, 38, 52, 93, 110, 183, 187
Democracy, 34, 66, 185, 188
Deontologists, 47, 135
Descartes, René, 6, 45, 83
Dichotomies, 17; fact-value, 95, 98–99
Disappointment, 150, 152, 167, 170
Diversity, 30, 33, 55, 71, 90, 97, 107, 118–119, 141
Domination, 69, 70, 74–75, 77, 113, 141, 153–154, 162, 163, 168–169, 181, 184, 186–187
Duty, 32, 33, 117, 139, 140, 141, 144, 146, 147, 153, 154, 156, 157, 168

Emotivists, 23
Enlightenment, 107, 136, 178
Epistemology, 10, 11, 18, 97, 103
Equality, 63, 184, 185, 187
Ergon, 29
Erotic feeling, 124–127
Evil, 8, 67, 75–78, 89–90, 106–107, 118–119, 147, 169, 170–171, 184, 186, 187
Expediency, 164, 168, 171

Fairness. *See* Justice
False fixities, 57
False isolation, 82–83, 85
Fanaticism, 99, 119, 136, 137, 146, 188
Fascism, 5, 6, 11, 71
Feminism, 56, 104
Fiction, 105
Florence, 35, 162

Fortune, 101, 163, 171
Freedom, 64, 106, 135, 184
French Revolution, 9, 66, 71, 167
Freud, Sigmund, 35, 126
Friendship, 55, 68, 74, 140, 154, 165, 166, 175, 187
Frontiers, moral, 135, 155, 156

Genocide, 69–71
Germany, 4, 5, 47, 67, 75, 76
Glory, 107, 161, 164–167, 174, 178
God, 39, 60, 70, 116, 130, 143, 144, 164, 174, 179
Good: attributive versus predicative use, 24, 106; conceptions of, 13, 17, 57, 64, 73, 90, 98, 100, 102, 103, 106–108, 113, 116, 117, 119, 124, 132, 134, 135, 139, 140–148, 153, 155, 156, 164–174, 177, 178, 180, 181, 183, 184, 186–189; predication by analogy, 105; primary, 68; supreme, 72
Gratitude, 138, 147, 148, 152, 163, 177

Happiness, 71, 106, 148–153
Harmony, 141, 143, 181, 189
Hegel, G. W. F., 6, 7, 66, 137, 141, 150, 178, 179
Heraclitus, 121, 182, 189
Hierarchy, 35, 37
Historical continuity, 73, 115, 138
Hitler, Adolf, 4, 5, 8, 75, 76, 89
Hobbes, Thomas, 35, 55, 60, 68, 73, 74, 82, 141, 157, 188
Holism, 122–123
Homer, 14, 46, 52
Hope, 11, 150, 151, 153
Humanity, 30, 44, 64, 106, 107, 114–116, 124, 131, 137, 140, 147, 148, 150, 179, 180
Human nature, 31–33, 42, 45, 71, 107, 157, 189
Hume, David, 17, 18, 23, 35, 77, 81–110, 121, 122, 138, 156, 157, 166

Identity: cultural and national, 73, 151; individual, 115
Ideology, 35, 38, 157
Imagination, 30, 31, 45–47, 115, 116, 118, 125–128, 130, 131, 133, 134, 137, 139, 147, 176
Immortality, 148–149
Impressionistic description, 96–98
Individuality, 114–118, 119, 123, 124, 130–131, 146, 147, 156, 178
Inexhaustibility of description, 88
Infidels, 76, 99, 135, 143, 144, 146
Innocence, 12, 77, 136, 149, 150, 151, 152, 167–177, 186
Integrity, 12, 148, 157, 165, 174, 175, 177, 186
Intention, 47, 51, 60, 66, 86, 93, 163, 186
Invention, 30, 31

Jacobins, 75, 135, 136, 183, 184
Jews, 68, 69–70, 77, 93
Judgment, 15, 53, 92, 110; versus factual statement, 84, 91, 92, 101, 127
Justice, 29, 32, 33, 53, 56, 57, 60, 61, 63, 66, 68, 70–75, 91, 108, 109, 114, 124, 140, 142, 143, 149, 162, 164, 167, 168, 172, 182, 185; 186; concept of, 64, 73, 114, 145, 157, 169, 184, 187; conceptions of, 13, 61, 63–65, 71, 75, 78, 133, 140, 184; procedural, 14, 17, 53, 61, 65, 68, 72, 74, 94, 108, 124, 135, 137–138, 140–142, 145–146, 154, 155, 164, 168–169, 171, 176, 183, 185–187; substantial, 55, 57, 65, 68, 108, 119, 153–154, 164–165, 169, 171, 183–185, 187–188

Kafka, Franz, 70
Kant, Immanuel, 34, 35, 47, 48, 72, 107, 108, 133, 157

Liberal, 68, 71, 73, 76, 77, 136, 137, 142, 143, 153, 154, 184, 187, 188

Liberty, 55, 71, 73, 188; concept of, 68, 106
Lop-sidedness, 27, 28, 134
Loss, 117, 124, 147, 168
Loyalty, 139, 146, 152, 175

Machiavelli, Niccolò, 8, 11, 12, 13, 17, 60, 68, 101, 161–189
Manichean error, 125–126
Marx, Karl, 66, 141, 150, 178, 185
Marxism, 5, 6, 7, 10, 71, 138, 179, 184
Memory, 37, 42, 43, 61, 114, 120–122, 127, 133–134, 137, 149, 151, 152, 173, 180
Metaphor, 3, 9, 34, 35, 37, 40, 46, 52, 60, 121, 139, 171, 181, 182, 186
Metaphysics, 7, 41, 76, 139, 144
Mill, J. S., 23, 34, 66, 67, 71, 77, 118, 136, 157
Modal judgments, 84, 87–89, 91, 92, 95, 98, 99, 109–110
Moore, G. E., 23, 67, 77
Morality, 75–77, 119, 136, 145, 156, 164, 167; conventional, 76, 108, 117, 139; destruction of, 75, 156; positive versus negative, 13, 72, 119; two aspects, 4, 77, 114, 135, 136; universal requirements of, 113, 117, 139, 142, 143, 187
Moral priorities, 26, 39, 91, 106, 171
Museum, 64–65
Myth, 45, 126, 142, 149, 151; social, 55–57

Nationalism, 6, 137
National Socialists. *See* Nazis
Natural kinds, 25, 105
Nazis, 5, 9, 66–68, 70–77, 153
Necessity, 74, 142, 162; biological, 106, 125; epistemic, 84, 99, 100; moral, 84, 99, 110; nomic, 84, 99; prudential, 99
Negative virtue, 68, 72
Negotiation, 54, 74, 75, 78, 114,

143–146, 154, 168, 169, 174–176, 182, 185
Newton, Isaac, 102
Nietzsche, Friedrich, 76, 156–157

Objectivity, 25, 36, 88, 91, 97, 109, 110
Order: cosmic, 60; natural, 56–57, 59; social, 60, 61, 134

Perfection, 26, 28, 115, 116, 153, 166
Plato, 6, 12, 23, 27, 31, 34, 35, 69, 71, 72, 107, 109, 135, 157, 177, 181, 182, 189
Pleonexia, 71
Positivism, 138, 179; Comtean, 7, 61; logical, 6
Possibilities, 14, 15, 16, 18, 59, 63, 75, 83, 100–105, 185
Practical wisdom, 94, 149
Precedent, 63, 75, 141
Presupposition, 16, 60, 83, 84, 86, 90, 91, 92, 100
Procedure, 54, 55, 63, 74, 75, 119, 143, 145, 146, 169, 176, 183, 187; adversary, 53, 145, 181; of public discussion, 71, 142
Progress, 5, 7
Proletariat, 37–38
Propositions, singular hypothetical, 16, 102
Proust, Marcel, 127–129, 130, 132, 148
Psycho-analysis, 152

Race, 69, 76, 77
Rationality, 4, 48, 53, 54, 74, 77, 108, 110, 143, 155
Rauschning, Hermann, 68
Rawls, John, 67, 71, 142, 187, 188
Realpolitik, 74, 76, 175
Reason: dominance of, 35, 38, 40–41, 46–47, 189; practical, 16–19, 34, 41, 47, 51, 56, 57, 60, 64, 74,

94, 110, 119, 143, 145–146, 148, 152, 155, 175, 181, 183, 187; theoretical, 16, 19, 41, 94, 119, 143
Redemption, 7, 146, 179
Regret, 15, 100, 101
Relativism, 13, 58, 62, 64, 179
Renaissance, 35, 165, 168
Renunciation, 167
Richelieu, Cardinal, 167, 176
Rights, 56–57, 141, 171, 178, 184, 185, 188
Roman Empire, 5, 167
Romantic movement, 47, 149
Rousseau, Jean-Jacques, 71, 135, 141, 183, 184
Russian Revolution, 9, 66–67

Scepticism, 13, 14, 17, 18, 81, 86, 87, 88, 91, 100, 136, 175
Security, 162, 171, 172
Semantic complexity, 84, 88, 91, 92, 99, 100
Shakespeare, William, 8, 60, 127, 147, 148
Sidgwick, Henry, 67, 77
Singularity, 115, 117, 118, 129, 130
Slavery, 56–59, 63, 64
Smith, Adam, 77, 157
Social contract, 14, 188
Socialism, 5, 9, 11, 184, 185
Soul, 27, 30, 34, 35, 37, 40, 45, 47, 52, 125, 129, 136, 141, 182
Spinoza, 35, 45, 181, 182
Stoics, 13, 64

Teleology, 67, 180
Thucydides, 157, 170, 178
Tocqueville, 66, 157
Tolstoy, 88, 89
Tradition, 131, 139, 142
Transcendence, 132, 138, 145, 148, 166, 176
Treachery, 10, 11, 168, 177
Truth, 7, 11, 16, 32, 34, 41, 77, 82, 119, 148, 180

Utilitarians, 47, 72, 76, 77, 90, 108, 117, 118, 135, 136, 147

Value, perception of, 95–98
Vermeer, 130, 153
Verum factum principle, 45
Vico, 45–46
Vienna Circle, 6, 8
Violence, 69, 71
Virtue, 26, 28, 29, 33, 69, 82, 108, 134, 139, 148, 149, 157, 164–166, 168, 171, 177, 178, 181, 187; negative, 68, 72, 164, 172; republican, 167

Way of life, 15, 33, 57–59, 73, 109, 138, 139, 141, 153–156, 170, 179, 180, 181, 182, 184
Will to destruction, 76